Contents

Introduction: Building a Business, Building a Life   v

1 Anyone Can Do It   1
2 The Myths of Entrepreneurship   9
3 Where to Find Your Great Idea   19
4 Bootstrapping Your Business   41
5 The Power of International Trade   63
6 The Internet: An Entrepreneur's Powerful
   Global Tool   81
7 The "Wow" Factor   91
8 Marketing Your Product   109
9 Reduce Risk by Reducing Inventory   119
10 Hiring Employees   127
11 Buying a Business and Franchising   139
12 Knowing What Your Business Is Worth   149
13 When Can I Quit My Day Job?   157

Conclusion: Determination Is Everything   167
Appendix: Low-Risk Businesses You Can Start Today   173
Index   187

Introduction

Building a Business, Building a Life

IT WAS NOT SUPPOSED TO BE this way. If you worked hard for your company, if you were loyal, energetic, and enterprising, you were not supposed to end up unemployed, watching television in the middle of the day in a house worth half the amount you paid for it, your 401(k) dwindling, bill collectors hounding, job applications—hundreds of them—silently unanswered.

At one point during the recent recession, more than 10 percent of the U.S. workforce was unemployed, with another 7 percent too discouraged even to look for work. One out of ten workers was deemed unnecessary through no fault of the worker, but because of insane risk taking by those who had everything at their disposal: legendary brand names, massive amounts of capital, and the smartest business minds money could buy.

In spite of those resources, their companies imploded. Companies like General Motors, which survived the Great Depression and whose very name was once synonymous with the U.S. economy, and companies like Lehman Brothers, Bear Stearns, and AIG collapsed all around us. Some, like GM, survived only with massive government help. Others were obliterated.

Executives of these huge companies were paid hundreds of millions of dollars yet ran their companies into the ground. Some even got giant bonuses in the aftermath of their excessive, disastrous risk taking. Meanwhile, millions of American workers who played by the rules were sent home, often without health insurance. Their talents, energy, knowledge, and resources were wasted. The worst of the recession may be behind us, but it should never be forgotten. The experiences should be seared into our consciousness. Never again should we be so vulnerable, so powerless over our own lives and futures.

Equally terrifying can be a midlife realization that you are trapped in a life, industry, job, or location you do not like. If you're managing to pay the bills and maybe even saving a little bit for the future but are working for a company you don't like and doing something you don't enjoy doing, you will begin to feel trapped. You will want more out of life.

A Different Path

Entrepreneurship offers a path that's different from the safe route of staying on course with a job you don't like. It's actually a safer path. Traditionally, entrepreneurs have been considered the world's big risk takers. They were the ones who quit their jobs, mortgaged the house, and went for broke, with "broke" often being the end result. This book is not about that.

Nor is it a book about how to start the next Microsoft or Apple in your garage. It is about low-risk entrepreneurship—how you can launch small but profitable businesses today. It is a book about how to build those businesses slowly, sustainably, with minimal risk. The lessons within these pages are practical and filled with real-life examples from authors Jim Beach and Chris Hanks, two experienced entrepreneurs who proved how, even in a college classroom, businesses can be started from scratch and turn a profit quickly in turbulent economic times and across international borders.

This book is also about setting realistic expectations for your entrepreneurship endeavors. We hope you already have a job, but our suggestions will be the same whether you are employed or unemployed. We feel greatly for you if you are unemployed. The main goal of this book, though, is to teach you how to start a business without risking whatever assets you may have, such as a house, savings plan, or health insurance. The way to do that is to work on starting your business during the sixteen hours a day that you are not at your job. In doing so, you will build alternative income streams to diversify your risk. Currently, if you lose your job, you lose 100 percent of your income. If you had a side business that generated a quarter of your income and lost your job, you would lose 75 percent of your income. And so on.

This side business will start very small, generating perhaps only $15,000 of revenue in the first year, but $15,000 might cover a mortgage payment during turbulent times. In year two, the business may grow substantially and get to $40,000 or $50,000 per year, and you may find it increasingly difficult to maintain your schedule at your still-held job. In the third year, you may make up to $70,000 and decide it's finally possible to quit your job and transition your part-time business to a full-time endeavor.

We realize that readers of this book, battered in the down economy, are likely to be in a hurry to start turning a profit right away. With that in mind, we hope you will take from this book practical information that you can immediately put to use. We are providing ideas for quick startups, with specific, detailed information about where to get new business ideas, how to finance them, and what steps to take first.

It is important to remember that entrepreneurship does not have to be a distant dream. Launching a business does not have to take years or even months. But first, you must quickly adjust your mind-set and realize you are just as qualified as anyone else to be an entrepreneur. You are probably more qualified than many of the executives who ran those previously mentioned Fortune 500 companies into the ground.

The Right Way

It's also important to launch a business the right way, the low-risk way. If we have learned anything from the recent economic collapse, it is that there is no such thing as getting rich quickly. Entrepreneurship is rarely glamorous. It takes hard work and persistence. Spending any money at all on pipe dreams is a waste. As we have learned from the recent recession, those kinds of businesses—flipping houses, day-trading stocks, etc.—are not sustainable.

If anyone tries to sell you a kit loaded with fancy DVDs and glossy circulars, run. Don't buy expensive business cards, business suits, or stationery; you won't be needing them when you're working online. There's no need to rent an office either; you can work out of your living room or basement instead. No need to install a business phone line; use your cell. You don't want to pay for an expensive website; buy a $59 off-the-shelf site. If your business requires equipment, rent it until you are making a healthy profit. Avoid up-front costs at all costs.

The landscape is littered with entrepreneurs who have put all their money into the trappings of success, the glamorous stuff, but not the stuff that matters—the real inventory that can be sold to paying customers. Understand that entrepreneurship is not about appearances. It is not about having a glass office and a title. Entrepreneurs do not care what others think of them. Instead, they care about creating a sustainable, profitable business.

If you are lucky enough to have a job, you will definitely want to keep it for now. A key component of low-risk entrepreneurship is building your business while still working a day job. The key is maximizing your time off the clock to build up your business. You will need to start setting your alarm clock an hour earlier, packing shipments in the basement, and dropping them off at the post office on the way to work. At lunch, you will have to get on your cell phone and talk to prospective clients. At night, instead of watching "American Idol," you will be drumming up more business. If it seems like a tough grind, you just have to remember to keep your eyes on the prize. There will come a time when your businesses have grown large enough that you can leave the day job—on your terms, on your timetable.

That wasn't a typo in that last sentence—the word was *businesses*, plural. We believe your goal should be to start several businesses. Just as you would not put all your retirement money in one stock, so you should strive to diversify your business portfolio as a way to minimize risk and increase earnings. Having multiple revenue streams is the ticket to a low-risk life. With the right approach, these businesses will be soon be humming, and you will be making more money than ever before. You will be working hard, but it will not feel like the drudgery of toiling unappreciated for a company that could, in one stroke of a pen or a quick tap on the keyboard, kick you to the curb.

Stop Wasting Your Time

Entrepreneurship, of course, is not for everyone. There are those who prefer the security of a steady paycheck, paid vacation, and the interaction with coworkers that a corporate job provides. But the price of that security may be your own upside potential, which is often stifled in the modern workplace atmosphere.

Start with the daily commute, which can easily total three hours daily in many cities. That is three hours a day sapped from whatever it is that you are capable of producing, financially and creatively. When you arrive at the office, there is the obligatory chatting around the coffee pot or water cooler. The 9:30 morning meeting starts at 9:45, and then there is another fifteen minutes of listening to the boss discuss his or her grandchildren, mountain house, or art collection. You emerge from the morning meeting at 10:45, bolstered by a little corporate gossip and perhaps a few good jokes. There is more water cooler talk and a stack of voice messages and e-mails to answer that came in while you were in the meeting.

Then it's time for lunch. Maybe you are the type who, wisely, brings lunch from home and eats at your desk. Many others can't resist the temptation of going out for lunch regularly. This involves dragging themselves back into their cars, fighting traffic, and possibly sitting through the waiter's perky recitation of the daily specials. They eat fattening food, ingest some company gossip perhaps, and drag themselves back through traffic to the office, bloated and sleepy. After lunch, more voice mails and e-mails piling up. More water cooler talk. Then another meeting, mandatory, about something that has nothing to do with the task at hand, some change in the personnel policy, or maybe it's a meeting of employee fire marshals whose job it is to evacuate the building in an emergency. Then the day is over, and it's time to drag yourself back to the parking lot, back into hellish traffic.

With all the distractions, it is a wonder any work gets done. Some might argue that as long as you are getting paid for this, why worry? Because it is not just your time that is being wasted. It is your life. Your future. Every hour wasted could have been an hour you devoted to maximizing your potential and your income.

Wasted time is only one of the many issues that can stifle your potential. There is age discrimination, against both the young and the old, that one boss you offended with an off-the-cuff remark ten years ago, the normal cliques that are endemic to any organization, and also the overall bureaucracy and lack of imagination that result from a homogenized corporate culture that often values spreadsheets and meetings more than bold ideas.

Entrepreneurship creates the opposite environment. When you are paid directly by what you produce each day, you will operate as efficiently as possible, or you will be out of business in short order. You will learn to accomplish in two hours what it takes eight to do in a corporate environment. The result is that you will have much more free time—time to spend on the sideline of your child's soccer game, time to drive to the beach every Friday morning, or time to earn even more money—as much as you want.

There are tens of thousands of possible small businesses and no significant barrier to starting them. It is possible to have a profitable business up and running in ninety days or less. We hope this book helps you secure your own future and write your own script. That is the entrepreneurial dream, except that it is not a dream. It is yours for the taking. Randy Brown is one of many entrepreneurs who discovered this truth.

The Story of Randy Brown

Randy worked for a large, prestigious law firm in downtown Atlanta, and the firm was glad to have him. He worked hard, and compared with the amount of money he saved the firm, his salary was a bargain. Randy started with the firm when he was nineteen, making $4.50 an hour as a messenger. He noticed one day that the mailroom staff was able to complete its work in a few hours, spending the rest of the day loafing downstairs at the coffee shop. Yet the messengers struggled to finish their work each day. Randy talked to his superiors and arranged it so that the mail staff helped with messenger duties after finishing their regular work. Randy was obviously not a popular guy with the workers in the mailroom, but the bosses thought he was great.

So they let him keep on working there, year after year, giving him torturously small raises. Before he knew it, Randy had been there nineteen years and by 2004 was making only $30,000 a year. The story of why corporate America so often treats ambitious, innovative employees that way is a subject for another book. Yet it should be pointed out that any company's, and any country's, greatest assets are its human resources, the Randy Browns of the world.

Randy looked up one day to find himself at midcareer and middle-aged, earning a salary barely enough to make ends meet, and in possession of a nice collection of Employee of the Month certificates but with very little cash in the bank. He worked hard and was innovative, but his family had to scrimp. The company took him for granted because he allowed it to do so. That is what happens when you have no ownership in the company. Partners in the law firm where Randy worked share equally in the profits because they are the owners, the voting members of the board. With that ownership come power and financial reward.

Randy had a different vision from the one mapped out so comfortably by the law firm's management. He became his own advocate, believing in himself and starting his own company. He did it the right way, the low-risk way, and he succeeded. Randy's energy, resourcefulness, and hard work no longer reward a giant and thankless law firm. They reward Randy and his family.

Toward the end of his nineteen-year tenure at the firm, Randy started taking classes at Georgia State University to complete his undergraduate degree. He became familiar with the entrepreneurship courses taught by Jim Beach and Chris Hanks, two of the authors of this book. Randy had already been thinking about starting his own business, but he had no idea what that business would be. An idea seemed like the most important ingredient, and he was missing it.

Inspiration came from two places. First, his wife, Quinn, who worked for an insurance company, was assigned to research the possibility of the company outsourcing some of its procedures to India. She spent several weeks constantly thinking and talking about outsourcing as a way to reduce costs for large insurance companies.

Randy decided to transition to an outsourcing business providing office services such as court reporters and couriers for various law firms. In his entrepreneurship classes, Randy had learned several lessons that made him think twice about planning for his new business. First, he was very concerned about the risk he would be taking, so one of the decisions he made was not to start the company immediately, but instead to slowly ramp it up over time.

This is a crucial point. Trial and error is a major part of the learning curve for an entrepreneur. You will learn by making mistakes. Don't expect your competitors to issue field manuals on how to succeed in your chosen field. Your competitors will silently watch you fail, and there should probably be no real expectation otherwise. They are under no obligation to teach you how not to fail. You have to learn that yourself. But if at all possible, make those early mistakes while you still have a safety net to catch you.

Keep your day job and your health insurance benefits until you learn how to make your business profitable. If you abandon your day job and recklessly start a new business, those early mistakes—and there will be early mistakes—can derail you much more easily, because you will have less of a financial cushion.

Using this low-risk strategy, Randy started a company in the middle of 2004. He knew hundreds of lawyers already practicing in the Atlanta area, and he contacted several of them and asked if he could replace their current employees or vendors and provide the same services for them, usually at a cheaper price. Randy was able to negotiate discounts based on volume with court reporters, document production companies, investigators, accountants, messenger services, and other vendors—and he was able to pass these savings on to his clients and make a profit in the process.

The perfect business is one that saves money for your customers, increasing their bottom line, while also providing you a decent living. Randy's first client was a one-person legal office that hired him to coordinate its messenger service and court reporting. Randy was able to keep his day job while coordinating these facilities during lunch and at night after work. This meant he was working close to fourteen hours a day, going to school at night, and also being a good father and husband. He continued building clients slowly for about eighteen months, until the beginning of 2006, when he left the law firm and started running his business full-time.

Working long days, nights, and weekends while starting your own company, all while keeping your day job until the new business pays off, might seem like a schedule you would dread. But that is frequently not the case. Entrepreneurship often produces a unique effect psychologically and even physically. There is an adrenaline rush that results from knowing that the fruits of your labor benefit you and your family. No boss is screaming at you. No personnel file records every petty slight from years past. When your good fortune depends solely on you, your self-confidence explodes.

Even your day job will likely become easier once you start a business on the side. You know it's only temporary. It is not a dead end. When the boss screams at you, in the back of your mind, you are thinking this will all be over in a few months when your own business can support you. The future looks bright because you can see the light at the end of the tunnel.

Very few entrepreneurs are couch potatoes. That is why entrepreneurship can actually make a difference in you physically. You will notice that entrepreneurs often walk with a spring in their step, full of self-confidence, because they have proven to themselves that they can succeed. They are hopeful because the future is unlimited, not capped. Time spent watching TV is replaced by time spent packing boxes, unloading and stacking inventory, and carrying boxes into the UPS Store.

Randy's first year of business in 2006 was not without problems. While he had some customers and was able to get by, the business was not growing quickly enough, and he was very discouraged about the inflow of new clients. This is 100 percent normal. Growth always comes slowly, and your patience will be tried. Randy confided in his professors about these problems and was surprised with the bluntness of the answer. Jim told him to call five lawyers every day and ask for their business, and it worked. Today, Randy will say the biggest mistake during the startup of his business was failure to focus enough on sales. When you have existing clients calling every day with work to be done and problems to be solved, it is easy to forget new-client acquisition. Chris and Jim recommend spending the *first* hour of every day on client acquisition, sales, or marketing.

Randy has a very good reputation, but many area lawyers did not know he was now on his own. So calling them was a great first step in building the business, given his marketing plan, which centered on making face-to-face pitches to law firms. While many lawyers did not need his service at that time, many called later to hire him for particular projects. Also, Randy joined several area associations of paralegals and lawyers and was able to advertise directly to the community through his memberships in those groups. By the end of his first full year in business, he was able to acquire three full-time and seven part-time clients. He had doubled his old salary in two years.

That is what entrepreneurship can do for you and what you can do for yourself. That is what we will show you in this book.

1

Anyone Can
Do It

A BELIEF COMMON AMONG WOULD-BE ENTREPRENEURS is that only a chosen few are cut out for this kind of work, and everyone else is destined for a life in the corporate grind. Some people think entrepreneurs have some genetic trait that makes them capable of taking big risks, skirting colossal failure, and achieving great success while all others are addicted to the security of a monthly paycheck and health insurance. But in helping thousands of people start their own businesses, we have discovered over and over again that this myth is simply not true.

We believe that anyone, yes *anyone*, can be a successful entrepreneur. People love to argue this with us, and they always lose. Exactly what skill is required for starting a business? Do you have to be smart? No. Most business owners are far from geniuses. Do you have to have earned some prestigious graduate degree? No. Education in the form of a degree is irrelevant if you have the proper tools for success in place. We challenge you to find any criteria that a person must have in order to become a successful entrepreneur. The only characteristic that comes close to being necessary is raw desire and drive, and anyone who has picked up this book has demonstrated the requisite desire. Successful businesses can be launched quickly and profitably out of your basement, in your garage, or even, as shown in the following example, in a college classroom.

How Timeless Chair Was Born

The world was in turmoil in the months after the September 11, 2001, terrorist attacks. It was a tense period, marked by a swooning stock market. Today uncertainty and fear are with us again, this time due to the recession that started with the bursting of the subprime-lending bubble in 2008. In the fall of 2001, Jim Beach was teaching entrepreneurship to graduate students at Georgia State University in Atlanta. The enthusiasm of the students was palpable, but the university, as large institutions so often do, had him teaching the course with a textbook of fifteen-year-old case studies. The students, already upset about paying $129 for an old textbook, could not relate to stories about Larry Ellison, Bill Gates, or Oprah Winfrey. They realized that replicating these careers was about as likely as winning the lottery, maybe even less likely. Instead, they were anxious to start their own small businesses after college, so they could avoid entering the draconian corporate world.

Jim had a different idea. Why not use the classroom as an entrepreneurial laboratory? Why not start a company in the classroom? He was so confident of success that he let students choose the product and the country. Jim would provide the startup capital. If the company did not make a profit by the end of the four-month semester, he would give every student an automatic A. Earlier in the class, Jim had told the students how hard the furniture business was, how low the profit margins were. So the students joked about potentially starting a furniture company. In what country? Pakistan, of course, which was right in the center of the post-9/11 conflict and therefore not exactly the optimum location for starting a new business venture. Jim accepted the challenge, and the clock started ticking.

As students researched the furniture industry in Pakistan, they discovered that the country also had a very large rug industry, mostly producing handmade rugs. Jim and the class came up with the idea of combining the rug industry and the furniture trade. They would buy antique Persian rugs (sometimes called kilim) direct from the markets of Pakistan, cut them up, and use the pieces as upholstery for chairs. By the fourth week of class, they had only just gotten the idea off the ground, so time was running short to turn a profit.

LESSON #1

The U.S. Department of Commerce Gold Key Service is the best place to start planning any international business.

Jim contacted the U.S. Department of Commerce (DoC) office in Pakistan. The DoC runs a program called the Gold Key Service, which introduces American companies to possible partners overseas. One of the federal government's best-kept secrets, this service helps American businesses flourish globally. The department asked several questions about the price range and quality expectations, so it could get a better focus on what types of furniture makers the class was looking for. Jim responded with the requested information, and two hours before class the next day, he received a two-page faxed response listing about twenty companies that might be able to satisfy the requirements. One of the students in the class was from Pakistan, and he was able to provide additional names based on information from his family.

During the fifth week of the class, the students gave their new enterprise a name, based in large part on the availability of the Web domain name (the name of a website). They called their business Timeless Chair—and registered the domain name timelesschair .com—because these were new chairs covered with old carpets, giving them a timeless look. (A quick point about naming your low-risk, high-speed entrepreneurship venture: You can spend months of your time and thousands of dollars hiring a marketing firm to come up with a name for your company, but if the Web domain name is already taken, you'll need a different Web address. It's better to check first for domain name availability and shape the name of the company around those that are available. A domain name can be purchased for a very small amount of money, often for as little as $10 a year, from domain name registration sites such as GoDaddy.com or Register.com.)

LESSON #2

Name your company by finding an available domain name on registration sites such as Register.com or GoDaddy.com.

After they decided on a name, Jim's students set out to obtain books on chair design so they could refine their product. Soon they chose two high-back chairs, a classic dining room chair, two overstuffed chairs, and a library reading chair to emulate. These designs were then faxed to the list of possible suppliers in Pakistan. Three companies quickly responded. Within twenty-four hours, one company had a sample chair constructed and agreed to ship it UPS air express. Meanwhile, the students started working on creating a company website—nothing fancy, using just a $59 standard template design.

The first sample chair that arrived was a disappointment. The kilim fabric was boring and rough, hard to sit on. The polyurethane coating looked dusty. After the class complained, the manufacturer agreed to find better-quality fabric. A representative visited the local market, took digital photos of forty to fifty carpet samples, and e-mailed them back to the class for review.

Jim, seeking to improve the look of the chairs, also shipped the manufacturer a can of higher-quality polyurethane from the United States. There was simply not enough time left in the semester to locate another polyurethane supplier, so Jim decided to ship it himself directly. The owner e-mailed back, saying he could be finished with the original order of eighteen chairs and about ten ottomans within two weeks. This was about the right number to fill one shipping container, a practical consideration that entrepreneurs need to constantly keep on their radar screen. Too much inventory would force the class to pay for an extra container. Too little would have forced them to pay for empty space on the ship. Jim also started contacting various shipping companies that said they could have the container to the class in Charleston, South Carolina, thirty-one days after that. In terms of winning the bet with the class, it would be very close. The class would need to sell chairs within a week of them arriving in America. Jim might have helped them with some of the ideas, but the students would have to do the heavy lifting on their own.

The cost of the finished chairs was only $375 each. The ottomans cost about $175 each. So the total original bill was just under $7,000 plus about $3,500 for the container and shipping charges, bringing the grand total to about $11,500 to get the chairs into Charleston. The chairs themselves, in the end, were absolutely stunning. The fabrics were smooth, with bright, vibrant colors and exciting patterns. The manufacturer used solid mahogany even in the interior of the chairs, and the quality of the woodworking was close to perfect.

They even produced the difficult Queen Anne chair leg that turns in two directions at once impeccably.

Jim advised the students to price the chairs at around $2,000 each, believing their uniqueness justified that price. That would also mean the class would need to sell only six chairs to make a profit and for Jim to win the bet.

From then on, it was all marketing. As soon as the website was built, complete with pictures of the chairs and ottomans from Pakistan, the class was ready to get the word out. The goal was to sell as many of the chairs as possible before they arrived in Atlanta. With that in mind, the class let it be known on the website that each chair was an individual work of art with a limited supply, and that the furniture would be sold on a first-come, first-serve basis. Since each of the chairs had a unique carpet pattern on it, buyers would have to act quickly to ensure they got the pattern they wanted.

From a list broker (a company that sells lists of every conceivable specialty), Jim purchased a list of eight thousand interior decorators in the United States, and the class e-mailed them a sales pitch about the chairs, complete with photographs. In the first twenty-four hours after the e-mail, the website received about five hundred visits. Quickly, most of the ottomans and a couple of the chairs sold— enough for Jim to win the bet. It was not the sales mix the students had predicted, leaving them with a huge shortage of their most popular product, the cheaper ottomans.

The chairs arrived in Charleston one day ahead of schedule, and after clearing customs, they were trucked to a warehouse in Atlanta. The shipments were sent out the same week as final exams took place, but by that point, the class had already conceded that Jim had won the bet and they would not be getting automatic As, so they were studying hard for the final exam. Ultimately, Jim kept the profits from the chairs, since he put up all the capital. The students got the

As. Although Timeless Chair is no longer operational as a business, the site is still up and visible at http://www.timelesschair.com if you want to see how beautiful the product was.

If They Can Do It, You Can, Too

This exercise proves that any person, working from home with little money, even in the most challenging of economic times and the most hostile and turbulent political climate, can create a company from scratch and turn a profit quickly. Furthermore, any person can do all that even while operating across international borders, involving different currencies, time zones, and cultures, as well as customs forms and other shipping paperwork.

There could have been few more difficult environments in which to start a company than Jim's class experienced, and the business you start will likely be far less complex. But the point is to adopt a mind-set that it can be done for a small amount of money in a short amount of time. More than anything, that is what we hope will be this book's major lesson. We have already introduced you to Randy, and you will meet many more entrepreneurs in the following chapters. They all have several things in common: most particularly, the initiative necessary to go to war to create the future they want and deserve. The only thing that distinguishes these people from anyone else is this initiative. They are not smarter, prettier, better educated, funnier, or more resourceful than anyone else in the world. But they have chosen to control their income streams, rather than live at the beck and call of a corporation.

When given the correct advice, anyone can break free and become his or her own boss. This process is repeatable and reduces risk in a way that will allow you to keep your health insurance. All you have to do is break it down into a series of manageable goals. Running a marathon seems totally impossible, for instance, but walking a mile seems doable for most people. Starting a billion-dollar company seems totally impossible, but supplementing your income with an extra $25,000 of income is doable by everyone. Anyone and everyone can do this, and if you read this book, you will be able to do it, too.

2

The Myths of Entrepreneurship

IN THE PREVIOUS CHAPTER, WE TRIED TO DISPEL the most common myth about entrepreneurship, the belief that entrepreneurs are born, not created. The truth is that there is only one basic requirement for entrepreneurship: the drive to succeed. Once you have that, all the rest can be taught. We will teach you the steps, and by taking the initiative to read this, you are taking the important first step. The other ingredients are simple: hard work and persistence. These attributes can conquer all other obstacles. They are not genetic traits but decisions you make. You can't decide whether to be left-handed or right-handed, but you can make a choice to work hard each day, to do whatever it takes to make your business thrive, and to never give up.

LESSON #3

Success is not a genetic trait; it is a decision you make.

Starting a Business in a Down Economy

The second major myth of entrepreneurship is that new companies thrive only in a good economy. This is totally untrue. There are, in fact, many advantages to starting a small business when times are tough, particularly if the entrepreneur takes the low-risk approach advocated in this book. A down economy reduces your competition. The inefficient companies die while the low-risk businesses survive and even flourish. A down economy forces you to have a lean, mean operation with no debt. Excess debt is a greater threat to a business than a slow economy. Your low-risk startup will not use debt and will have positive cash flow early on. If you need proof, just look to us—the authors of this book—who have started profitable businesses in a down economy.

Chris Hanks started his first business to pay for college, largely because the jobs he found didn't pay enough to cover tuition. First, he hawked T-shirts in the dorm rooms. Then, after applying for a job delivering flowers, he realized that all the flower shops in town delivered to the same places—the churches, hospitals, etc. Soon enough, he had contracts with four shops to deliver their flowers, thus eliminating the need to hire additional staff. The business cost nothing to start and had zero risk. By delivering for four different shops, he reduced risk even further. After all, if he lost one shop at that point, he still had others to work for. The state of the economy was completely irrelevant to his success. People get sick in bad economies, and flowers must be delivered. It's a recession-proof industry—one of many.

Jim Beach started his first business, which provided technology training for young people, because he could not get a job during the recession of the early 1990s. He had made a lot of mistakes with his education, it turned out. Jim was trained to be a Japanese business professional and to live in Japan. He even spoke passable Japanese, but after living in Japan for two years, he found he didn't like it. So he was stuck with minimal job opportunities in areas he didn't want to pursue. He realized that perhaps he had to do something on his own.

In search of a solution, Jim and a friend, Doug Murphy, sat down one day and tried to think of a good business to start. Doug was also underemployed, having just finished a contract working as a Spanish translator for Ted Turner's Goodwill Games. Both of these men needed work, and they had the drive to want to start a business. Could they wait to get started until two years later, when the economy was likely to have improved? No, they needed to support themselves at that moment, and they did, as you will see later in this chapter.

Advantages of a Down Economy

Surprisingly, there are many advantages to starting a business in a down economy. Remember back in the late 1990s, when you could sell anything to anyone? It was easy to sell stuff then. So you didn't know if your product was good or if you were just benefiting from a hot economy—it didn't matter, your product was most likely getting sold. But then, in 2001 and especially 2002, it became very difficult to sell things. It was probably about as difficult as it is now. The companies with great products and services suffered but survived. The companies with weak products and services died a painful death.

Here's the main advantage, though: If you start a company during the good times, the flaws in the company are less likely to show. You don't know if your product is great, if the service you are offering is superior, or if sales are the result of a strong economy. In contrast, learning to sell your product during a bad economy is a blessing, because you will learn to sell it well. If something isn't working, you will know about it immediately and have the chance for a course correction. You become reliant on the superiority of the product, not the strength of the economy.

LESSON #4

When you start a business in a boom economy, your flaws might be hidden and therefore go unresolved.

When you start a business in a down economy, you will know immediately what isn't working, and you will have the chance to fix it.

Another advantage of starting a business in a down economy is that it is hard to find financing when times are tough. This may sound counterintuitive, but easy money has often been the kiss of death for companies. It encourages companies to grow too quickly, to accumulate excess inventory, staff, and overhead costs. We advocate starting a business with very little money, a pay-as-you-go approach called "bootstrapping," which will be discussed in more detail later in the book.

Bootstrapping is at the core of our philosophy of low-risk entrepreneurship. It means starting small with little or no overhead or debt and building slowly over time as sales and profits increase. You let your sales and profits, not debt, pull the company up. You should start your business with $5,000 or less. Doing so forces you to create a business slowly, sustainably, without taking on excessive debt or overhead. It may limit your upside potential early on, but it lowers your risk in the short and long term. You will not be an instant millionaire, but you will have a sustainable, long-term business that will provide you and your family with a comfortable living and can be sold or passed on to your children when you retire.

Also, starting a new business during bad times forces you to be more persistent. It makes you hungry; it forces you to go out there and sell harder, focus on strategy, and hustle—which is all going to make your product and your sales pitch better overall. If you have to sell your product or service in order to eat or make your mortgage payment, you are going to work so much harder, and that will make you better at the tasks you've set out for yourself. If you learn to sell a product today, when times are bad, how easy is it going to be to sell when times are good?

When times are tough, you're not going to make the mistake of hiring a big staff, importing expensive office furniture, and spending $3,000 on a professionally designed company logo. Indeed, in these times, you will be more inclined to make your resources go a long way. When and if you do hire someone to help you with your business, a down economy is actually a great time to find good people at low costs. It's very likely you'll be offering a job to someone who used to make $60,000, and saying, "I can't pay you that much, but we will give you $40,000 and some shares in the company." In a tough economy, people are more willing to work hard for less money, because they will be thankful to work at all. When you hear about people getting laid off, you can hire them, and you have an opportunity to cherry-pick the very best people. You can get a better staff for much less money during the bad times.

Finally, during economic slumps, big companies often reduce their spending on research and development. They pull back from promising markets. This gives smaller companies an opening that would probably not exist in the boom times. You are more likely to find voids in the market—products or services that are not being offered by the big companies.

Reducing the Risk of Your New Business

Let us now consider another myth about entrepreneurs—that they are all risk takers. Wrong! Entrepreneurs want to hedge their bets as much as anyone else. Let's play a game. Assume you've gone on vacation in Mexico to lie in the sun and knock back a few drinks with umbrellas in them. You go to the beach one day, enjoy the sun and the surf, and have a wonderful time. Later in the day, your wife comes to you and says she would like to see the cliff divers. She has heard about the wonderful show they perform and the amazing risks they take. So you join the crowd at the cliff-diving demonstration, and they introduce their star cliff diver, José. He has been diving for thirty-two years and is the most famous diver in all of Mexico. Before every show, José spends three hours getting prepared, all just so he can jump off a cliff.

When you arrive at the show and buy your ticket, the waitress comes and offers more drinks with umbrellas in them. Let's pretend, though, that at this performance, the emcee comes out and invites someone from the audience to participate in the show. He claims it is safe and easy, and furthermore, it will be fun! For some reason that would probably be best left unexamined, your wife raises her hand to volunteer for you. "Take a risk," she says to you. "If he can do it, you can do it!" Perhaps because you have ingested so much of the bravery juice already, you agree to this plan and head up the hill to the top of the cliff.

Let's look at the difference in this situation between José and yourself. What has José done all day? He has prepared. He fed the shark that lives in the landing pool, so it won't be hungry. He has stretched and exercised, and he's ready to go. What does José know? He knows about the big rock hiding in the water that he must avoid. He knows that when the water swells fifty yards offshore, that is the time to jump because in the two or three seconds that it takes to fall from the top to the water, that swell of water will come in, and the water will be the deepest when you need it. How long has José been doing this? He's been doing it his entire life.

Who is our risk taker, the cliff diver or you with your umbrella drinks? You are, of course. You are doing something new and exciting and risking your life. Who is the entrepreneur? José. He did his research. He knows his industry. He knows the lay of the land. He is patient, persistent. In any way possible, he reduces the risk of the endeavor until starting the business is no longer a risky activity.

Meanwhile, you go bankrupt—right against that huge rock hiding just beneath the surface of the water.

Entrepreneurship and risk do not necessarily go together. Someone who takes a lot of risk is called a daredevil, and daredevils are rarely confused with entrepreneurs.

What Is at Risk

Before launching your business, ask yourself this question: what am I risking as an entrepreneur? The list could include money, of course, but also your time, relationships, reputation, and even your health.

But the most important message of this book is that your strategy from day one should be to minimize all those risks.

Are you willing to risk $5,000 to start a business? Sure, that's not so risky. Most people can't afford to spend $50,000, $100,000, or $1 million, and it's probably for the best that they can't. It is important to build slowly, to reduce risk, and to save money. You are going to keep your desires and fantasies in check, and you'll start a small business that makes sense.

LESSON #5

The less you risk in your business, the less you stand to lose.

Time

Entrepreneurs may temporarily have to give up certain luxuries, such as going out to eat, watching movies and television, reading frivolous magazines, and checking out Sunday football games. We ask our students all the time, "How many of you waste fifteen or twenty hours a week on frivolous activities that could easily be cut in order to start your business?" Almost all of them admit to wasting time in many aspects of their lives.

Health

Entrepreneurs work crazy hours. Many of them tend not to focus too heavily on finding the best meals when they get a chance to eat. They might not be well rested either. Let's face it, in one way or another, when you start a new business, you are putting your health at risk. You're going to want to listen to your mother on this one, though, and keep as healthy as possible. Do not allow your business to become all-consuming, which is a temptation for all entrepreneurs. Do not become obsessed with your business. Allow time for your family and time for sleep. Do not let the business destroy your relationships or your health. That is too high a price to pay for business success.

Your Company Doesn't Have to Be Unique

The final myth of entrepreneurship is that to start a successful business, you have to have a unique idea—an idea that nobody else in the entire universe has ever dreamed up before. If that were true, though, the number of businesses currently thriving would be drastically reduced overnight to next to nothing.

Would you be upset if you were the one who started Burger King, Dell, Adidas, PepsiCo, or Hyatt? Probably not. There's always a secondary player that's a strong competitor to the industry leader. Those companies make a lot of money, too. What if your sibling, son or daughter, or spouse started a business that was sort of like another business but not exactly the same? Would you think of that person as less cool because the business is similar to someone else's? It depends on the results, doesn't it?

LESSON #6

Your business does not have to be unique. You can learn from the successes and failures of others in order to become their competitors.

Nobody will judge you for what your business is if you do it well and if it is profitable. Seeing a good idea and borrowing it is fine. The primary source of ideas is borrowing from others. According to the Global Entrepreneurship Monitor, 93 percent of businesses worldwide are copied from existing businesses. There is nothing wrong with that! Borrow an idea from someone else, and execute it better.

Jim and Doug's company was called American Computer Experience (ACE). It started off as a computer camp, and in the next seven years, it grew into an industry leader, teaching technology to kids. It started as a blatant copy of someone else's camp. The competitor's camp was held at an old 1950s summer resort, while Jim and Doug held theirs at MIT and Stanford University and eighty other brand-name schools. The competition charged $365 a week. Jim and Doug figured out a way they could charge $850 a week and, more important, make sure each student got his or her money's worth. The higher price actually added to the perceived value of the product, making it more valuable simply by being more expensive. The "cool factor" allowed them to charge more: "What's your son doing this summer?" "Oh, he's studying computers at no less than Stanford University."

Also, the competition had no corporate sponsorships. Jim and Doug hustled hard, and eventually they lined up for ACE's corporate sponsors Intel, Microsoft, and most of the other large technology companies. All told, Jim and Doug had put together a computer training program for kids with locations at MIT and Stanford, sponsored by Microsoft and Intel. They had surrounded themselves with credibility, and in doing so, they made their competition obsolete.

The difference was execution: Better venues. Better partners. Better price positioning. Better teachers. More fun. Bluer sky. Cleaner air. They took an idea and made it a lot better. Low-risk entrepreneurs have license to copy a good, proven idea from others, execute it conservatively, and execute it with skill.

By now, you should see the possibilities all around that exist for you to start your own business. Don't be fooled by any of the myths surrounding entrepreneurship. There is not one good reason justifying your inactivity. Start now! In the next chapter, we will show you how to find your business idea.

3

Where to Find Your Great Idea

IT'S AN UNFORTUNATE TRUTH OF LIFE: creativity is beaten out of us as we age. When you are a kid, you are supposed to be creative, and you're encouraged by teachers with creative art projects where you get to draw whatever you want. But then you start designing a three-headed monster, and someone, maybe a brother or teacher, tells you, "But monsters only have one head." Over time, the innovation and creativity of youth disappear. As we get older and go to school, we seem to become less and less creative as our lessons become more about data and processes. Certainly, law school and business school are designed to beat the creativity out of you. By the time you graduate, you might forget what it was like to envision a monster with three heads.

We have so many rules in society that you tend to look silly if you have a new idea. Most of the time, you will be encouraged quickly, in one way or another, to fall back in line. Almost all of the new great ideas have been met with laughter. Even great ideas that *aren't* new are met with laughter, too. After all, someone surely laughed at the Pepsi-Cola Company for daring to go against Coca-Cola. How then do we overcome this resistance to new ideas and find the bolt of lightning that sparks our creativity?

Re-Create Your Current Occupation

Probably the easiest way to find a business idea is to look at your current occupation and see if you can replicate it on your own. Eric Joiner worked for Lockheed, the aircraft manufacturer, in the late 1960s and developed a love for selling and working overseas. Before he even graduated from college, he was selling C-100 airplanes around the world. Fortunately for him, Lockheed had a requirement that employees had to be at least thirty-five years old before they could become a manager, so Eric left the company, hoping to make his way up the corporate ladder sooner in a different form. He went into the shipping business, where he eventually took on a customer that bought and sold chickens around the world.

LESSON #7

One of the best ways to start a business is to focus on your current occupation and do it on your own, better than your bosses do it.

Although the company he worked for was in trouble and eventually failed, what Eric got from this experience was the certainty that he could do the same thing on his own. At the age of twenty-eight, Eric and his friend Gerald Allison started a company called AJC International. The company bought and sold chicken parts around the world. They started with a $1,000 investment and today, about thirty years later, have a company with twelve offices around the world, over three hundred employees, and over $1 billion in annual sales.

David Stahl is another example of the same principle. At only thirty-two years old, David is still pretty young, but that hasn't impeded his success. He went to school to become a software developer, and during the dot-com craziness, David and several friends ended up working for a venture-capital-funded software firm. There were clashes between the owners and investors, and eventually David and his friends were let go as the firm slowly disintegrated. Since the old company no longer existed, David and two of his friends saw an opportunity.

The three then pulled out their Rolodexes and called some of their past clients and college buddies looking for work. Interestingly, instead of trying to get jobs individually, they worked as a team, offering the services of all three programmers to these new potential clients. Soon they were able to secure a three-month contract doing software development. Their plan was to do contract work until they could find other jobs, but they discovered that it was easier to get contracts than it was to find a job. By the end of the fourth year, the company, called Infinovate, had seventeen employees and, with almost no marketing dollars, produced $2.5 million in revenue. They took the valuable skills they had acquired in the corporate world and made them even more valuable by working for themselves, cutting out the middleman, greatly increasing their potential income. That is perhaps the most important and lucrative benefit of entrepreneurship.

Follow Your Passion

Even though it's a solid idea to start a new business based on the current work you do, you obviously wouldn't want to do that if you were sick of your current job and wanted to try your hand at something else. If you're sick of your job and you try to start a new venture based around it, you are probably dooming yourself and anyone else involved to failure. One of the most important factors in starting a new business is passion. If you are looking for an idea of what kind of business you should start, look toward your passion.

Joey Tatum, Jason Wilson, and Catherine Simpson are entrepreneurs who started their businesses because of a deep passion for their work. They are all the type of people who are good workers for someone else but are great workers when their work determines their paycheck. They all love what they do, and they prove that people are willing to work eighty hours a week when they work for themselves.

Joey's Story

After getting a degree in sociology, Joey's first job was as an intern in New York City, working as a fashion designer. Looking at Joey, you would not take him for a fashion designer; his wardrobe could be described as garage sale chic. To help you get a sense for the type of person that Joey is, you would need to visit his lake house, which he recently purchased for his wife and twin two-year-old girls. The house, located on one of the fashionable lakes in North Georgia, consists of three yellow school buses welded together to create a home.

Joey grew tired of fashion and New York City fairly quickly and bounced around several jobs in the food service industry for six or seven years. What he realized while working this string of jobs was that his true passion was for bars. Something about the convivial atmosphere of a bar and the loyalty of regular customers made Joey want to own one. Of course, this is a business plan that so many people have; it has become a cliché to aspire to start a bar or restaurant. According to RestaurantOwner.com, 27 percent of restaurants fail in the first year, 50 percent fail by year three, and 70 percent fail by year ten. So for Joey and all of the other countless men and women who have wanted to start a bar or restaurant, their odds of succeeding are very low.

Perhaps not knowing better, Joey felt that he could succeed where others had failed. His passion pushed him forward, even though common sense would have told him to resist the temptation. Joey started saving every penny he could and became a regular in several bars in the Athens, Georgia, area. In 1993, almost all of the bars in town were for University of Georgia college kids. Only one or two bars were for locals, and these establishments did not go out of their way to make you feel welcome. Joey saw room for a true "townie bar."

He began scouting for locations and soon found a bar that was operating almost as the landlord's personal playhouse. The landlord ran this small bar mostly for his friends, and it was open only three or four hours per day. Joey went out of his way to get to know the man, and six months later, Joey signed a lease for the space. Today, fifteen years later, Joey owns two bars, a restaurant, two rental houses, a parking lot, and several retail buildings. Joey identified his passion, ran with it, and wrote his life's script around that passion, rather than have someone else write it for him. Entrepreneurship gave him that power and those options.

Jason's Story

Another success story is Jason Wilson, a man who, like Joey, is passionate about beer. Jason worked for a large building-products manufacturer as a logistics specialist focusing on plywood and lumber. He had a tough time turning thirty. It hit him like a ton of bricks. Jason grew up in Gadsden, Alabama, and like many southerners, he is obsessed with his genealogy and is currently hooked on Ancestry.com.

In 2001, Jason went to Colorado to ski with his brother, a ski instructor. At some point during the trip, they went to a brewery pub. Having just turned twenty-one, Jason was struck by how delicious the Red Lady Ale was. He'd grown up drinking light beer, and this ale was the best beer he had ever consumed. The man next to him turned around, thanked Jason, and introduced himself as the brewer. This man was responsible for every stage of the process with ultimate control, from raw materials to the temperature of the glass the beer was served in. Jason realized at that moment that he wanted to make his own beer. Unlike the big breweries, which try to convince millions of people to like the same beer, Jason wanted to make a beer that catered to specific groups of individuals. The passion became clear, although it took him almost a decade for it to materialize.

Jason spent several years studying breweries and beer companies, and instead of focusing on the successes, which we see all of the time, he decided to focus on what caused all of the others to fail. He learned that at year two, many companies fail because they do not have enough funding. At year five, they fail because they run out of passion and get tired. Jason vowed to never let this happen and soon started the Back Forty Beer Company with his first product: Naked Pig Pale Ale. The "back forty" is an agricultural term that refers to the forty acres farthest from the barn. Usually fertile soil, this acreage is the hardest to maintain and irrigate and is not frequently used. Only a farmer willing to overcome all the obstacles grows on the back forty.

In its first nine months of operation, Back Forty Beer Company sold five thousand cases in 450 retail locations across Alabama, with $500,000 in revenue. Jason is another example of someone who combined sustainable passion for a product with a slow, methodical buildup of the company, starting small with money he had saved from other jobs. The company is still going strong, winning a silver medal in the 2010 Great American Beer Festival in Denver.

Catherine's Story

Catherine Simpson comes from a very successful and educated family. Her father has a Harvard MBA, and her mother runs a successful art gallery. Catherine went to Georgetown University and got a degree in social work in 1989. She has long blond hair and is a single mom with a beautiful four-year-old girl. As a very strong advocate of animal rights, the environment, and equality for minorities, she grew up wanting to do good for other people. She rallied against big business on the behalf of workers, and claimed not to care about money.

When she graduated from college, she moved to San Francisco and got a job doing social work helping disadvantaged children.

On the surface, that job certainly seems perfect for Catherine, as it allows her to help a disadvantaged group. But out of the blue, and without being able to explain why, she became disenchanted with it all, quit her job, and left San Francisco to move in with her parents. What happened next is one of the strangest entrepreneur stories that we have run across, but it nevertheless demonstrates how passion can be such a driving force in coming up with a blueprint for business success.

What happened was this: Catherine started an automobile repair business. At one level, this shocked her friends beyond words. What was a liberal, vegan, blond girl doing running an automobile garage? On another level, it made a lot of sense. Catherine just wants to fix things in the world. She loves to solve problems for other people and wants to make the world a better place. Although social work is clearly the more noble profession, the results are less certain. You might work with a child for fifteen years and still not "fix" the child or even make him or her happy. With an automobile garage, when the car owner drives out of the parking lot, you can safely say the car has been fixed.

Catherine soon realized that business owners really can make a difference. They may not be able to enact broad, sweeping change through legislation, but they can help people on an individual level get on with their lives. Her goal now is to change how all people get car repair done. She may not have a passion for cars, but in working with them, she realized she had a big opportunity to exercise her passion for fairness. That is, she now gets to make sure that women don't get cheated by auto mechanics, she makes sure that her employees get great benefits, and she helps an industry known for dishonesty have at least one sterling example of integrity.

Joey, Jason, and Catherine love what they do. They have a passion for their industries and would gladly go to work every day even if they weren't getting paid. Sometimes, the exact business an entrepreneur runs is secondary to the passion that drives and motivates them.

You Are Your Ideal Customer

Aside from being passionate about what you do for a living, you should also be passionate about the product specifically. When you are trying to figure out what kind of business to go into, one solid strategy is simply to think about providing exactly the kind of service that you would use yourself.

Someone who fits this mold to a T is Jeff Galloway. Jeff knew he always wanted to be a teacher, and in fact, his father was a very respected high school educator and started a private school in Atlanta, the Galloway School, which is going into its forty-second year of operation. Jeff was also a runner and competed in the 1972 Munich Olympics. One of Jeff's friends was the third employee at a new company, a little company you may have heard of called Nike. This friend was opening a runners-oriented sporting goods store in Oregon, and Jeff saw this store as a great way to remain competitive at the world-class level. It was the kind of store he wanted to shop at, so it made sense to him that it would be the kind of place he'd want to have as a business. Jeff, along with a college professor friend of his, opened their first store in Tallahassee with an initial investment of $5,000.

The store was named Phidippides, after the first man to run what is now called a marathon. The store did $51,000 in sales in its first year, and neither owner took a salary for two years. Another store was soon opened in the Atlanta area. The main premise of the store was not to make money but to provide service to local runners. All of the employees were very well trained and, as runners themselves, were able to provide very specific advice. For example, an employee might ask a customer to run up and down the sidewalk so the employee could observe the customer's style and body position in order to select the perfect shoe for that individual. Jeff believes there is a shoe that fits each runner the best, which will prevent injury and therefore keep runners more interested in the sport.

The stores have had their ups and downs, and eventually the two partners split, with the friend taking the Tallahassee store and Jeff keeping the Atlanta store. In the 1980s, Jeff sold about thirty franchises, of which only a handful survive. Through the trials and tribulations of running a retail establishment, Jeff saw his true calling, one that would allow him to be a teacher in a way, provide a definite service to others, and keep him running at a competitive, world-class level.

In 1985, Jeff created a company called Galloway Productions to focus on running clinics, camps, and schools. Galloway Productions has trained more than 250,000 runners, has five full-time employees, and allows Jeff to be one of the most prominent running experts in the United States. He gives over 250 motivational talks a year, has a free monthly newsletter that goes out to over 70,000 people, writes monthly magazine articles, has written eighteen books, which have sold over 850,000 copies, and answers hundreds of e-mails a day to encourage other runners. At sixty-four years old, Jeff still runs a marathon almost every month and has fulfilled his dreams of teaching others. Forty years after starting his entrepreneurial journey, he embodies the business founder who has made lots of money simply trying to provide a service that helps others in a way he would want to be helped.

What's Popular Now?

Of course, not everybody can be so self-directed. Sometimes it's best to take a look around and see what's going on in the world in order to figure out what kind of business to go into. Simply going after your interests is a solid strategy, but so is going after the interests of others. You can capitalize big in this way by focusing on the trends you see around you. When you are standing on the sidelines of your child's soccer game, talk to other parents and subtly guide the conversation to the hottest new trends and products. Or just listen quietly in the background to other conversations, and make a mental note of what's being buzzed about.

Cherie Stine is a suburban mom. She has a marketing background, and in September 2009, she and her friend were having coffee and talking about Malcolm Gladwell's great book *The Tipping Point*. A tipping point, Gladwell says, occurs when an idea, trend, or social behavior crosses some imaginary threshold and begins to spread like wildfire. Just as one sick person can start an entire epidemic, one precisely targeted campaign can start a fashion trend, particularly with a new product, that becomes the rage of an entire society. Cherie and her friend were talking about their children and the current obsession of kids to wear shaped rubber bands around their wrists.

The stores in their neighborhood were constantly running out of the rubber bands, and the women saw an opportunity. Starting small, which as we have said is how you reduce risk, they thought opening a mall kiosk to sell the product for just seven weeks in November and December would be a safe bet. They did a little research and were able to secure a large supply up front, putting the entire cost on a credit card. They believed they could get better inventory and keep the merchandise in stock because they bought higher quantities up front.

A week after their kiosk opened in the mall, the two friends had to buy stanchions to keep the lines under control. The lines had gotten so long that they reached out of the mall and out into the parking lot, landing them on the local TV newscast. The reporters tried to understand where the trend started, and some even gave these two women complete credit for having started the trend themselves, when in fact they were simply filling a demand they had already seen develop in their own children. In November, they opened their second kiosk, and by the time they closed on New Year's Eve, they had sold over forty-two thousand packs of rubber band bracelets. The company, Stretchy Shapes, is a competitor to Silly Bandz and has annual revenues of $7 million in only its first full year of operation.

In future chapters, we will tell you a lot more about Cherie and her incredible successes. For now, though, just remember that if you keep your eyes open and your ear to the ground, you might come up with the next big thing before it becomes a thing at all.

Solve a Problem

Sometimes entrepreneurs give birth to great ideas for businesses by coming up with solutions that are profitable. Problems can inspire entrepreneurs to create brilliant new products that solve significant problems in the world. A great way to come up with the creative spark for your business is to think about somebody's problem and how you might be able to get to the bottom of it. One such problem was that of dogs who are afraid of thunderstorms.

Ben's Story

Ben Feldman received both undergraduate and master of business administration degrees from Duke University. Ben, unlike most of our other success stories, comes from a family of entrepreneurs. He started his first business in Washington, D.C., recycling glass bottles from bars. The business failed because of intense competition from Waste Management Inc., but he learned a lot of lessons from the experience. The industry was too big, and the competitors too strong. It was not a niche market, and from these experiences, he developed a manifesto of entrepreneurship, which advocates going into a niche that is not getting much attention, not big enough to have big players or attract them in the future. As Chris Hanks, one of the authors of this book, has said for years, "There are riches in the niches!"

After graduate school, Ben joined a software company with venture capital backing. He was the marketing director and worked about ninety hours a week. As he desired a better work-life balance, the job did not last long.

But let's get back to dogs that are afraid of thunderstorms. Ben's golf buddy Phil had a dog that, as you can now guess, was afraid of thunderstorms. Phil gave the dog drugs, which did not help. Through a little bit of research, Ben learned of a woman who had developed a pressure blanket for cows to calm them when they were being vaccinated or slaughtered. Ben was able to get samples from Mexico, created a cheap website, and started selling dog blankets in May 2009. He bought ads on Google and attended shows for dog trainers and veterinarians, getting them excited about the product. He ended up selling one hundred units in the first month alone. Then he went to the Global Pet Expo in early 2010 and was declared runner-up for best new pet product of the year. The company has already experienced several million dollars in sales.

Ben's business is thriving because he is solving a consumer's problem. This is another area to listen out for in conversations with friends and family. When they talk about an impossible problem with no readily available solutions, there might just be a business idea there.

Paul's Story

A business can be as simple as a tool in your garage. During a horrific ice storm in 1973, Paul Paulson had an idea: go to Sears and buy a chain saw. He drove through wealthy neighborhoods, cutting fallen limbs and making a killing from grateful residents who were finally able to get out of their driveways. That launched a lifetime business that eventually led to stump grinding. Paul, a Georgia State University graduate, and his wife, Betty, worked together, making good money and stashing money into a brokerage account, retiring comfortably to a life of frequent cruises and other travel and hobbies.

The same type of business could be launched with a snow blower, a wood splitter, a pickup truck, a sewing machine. Even if used only seasonally, this is another revenue stream, another business.

Terri's Story

Of course, while you're out there solving all of the world's ills, pay attention to your own problems, and see if you can't solve them, too. For Terri Alpert, a lucrative business was launched from something as simple as trying to find a decent chef's knife for her husband as a present. In the 1980s, Terri worked on Wall Street, where she felt there was an entitled group of people who had no idea what money was truly worth. Terri decided to use her maternity leave from Morgan Stanley as an opportunity to study entrepreneurship and see if she could find a business that would provide her with a sense of fulfillment.

At first, though, things did not go well. The move was difficult, and Terri encountered some problems. She ended up in a dark apartment with a colicky baby and no sense of self-worth. In Terri's depressed state, she went for a drive to escape the baby, dark apartment, and self-doubt, and she ran across a nice store. Her husband wanted a chef's knife set as a present, and he and Terri had done a lot of research on knives. "I've always been a synthesizer of large amounts of information, as long as the subject interests me, and I've loved being my husband's sidekick on these searches," Terri said.

At the same time, she was searching for a niche product to sell. Unfortunately for the store she entered that day, she knew more than the salespeople, and their selection was horrible. She experienced the same problem at other stores. "Again and again, we found that the people trying to sell it to us didn't know very much," she said. "All they knew was that whatever they sold was the best, but they couldn't tell you why and couldn't make intelligent comparisons about the differences among the brands." This is when Terri's creativity kicked into gear. If she was having such a hard time finding a good knife, surely other people were having the same problem. It seemed as though she had accidentally discovered a niche.

Terri launched a company called Professional Cutlery Direct in 1993, starting with an ad in *Food and Wine* magazine, featuring a forged eight-inch chef's knife from Switzerland (the very knife her husband decided to buy for its quality, value, and French shape). Terri was not even sure the magazine had hit the newsstands yet when she got her first order over the telephone. "After I hung up the phone, I went to the other room and got my eleven-month-old baby from the playpen, held her tight, and jumped up and down and in circles, saying, 'We are in business, Sarah-Bear. You and me! We are in business!'"

In the first few years, she took many of the orders herself over the telephone. Her mother also helped. Nearly eighteen years later, the company has more than $11 million a year in revenue, has been listed in several magazine "top 500" lists, and employs fifty-three people. "Even on the days when we ship three thousand packages or more, we put a handwritten note on every packing list, every time," Terri said.

It all started with a problem Terri encountered in the market-place—few stores selling high-quality cutlery. Most of us encounter situations like that all the time. You just can't find the product or service you need. Keep that in your mind-set always, and also try to elicit similar problems from your friends and relatives. Therein lies opportunity.

LESSON #8

Don't second-guess yourself so much! If you have an idea you are confident in, get started right away at getting your business off of the ground. Don't overthink it.

Turning on the Lightbulb

After you finish reading this chapter, there may still be no light bulb. You are still sitting in the dark, saying, "Well, those sure are cute stories, and I wish I were one of those people, but I still don't have an idea!" You are surely not alone. There are a lot of ways to get your inspiration, though.

Try this approach. When you see a product you admire in a store, consider selling that product yourself. Look up the company's website, and see if you can find out how to buy wholesale, how to become a dealer. This is not an exclusive club. Companies want more dealers, and many understand that starting small, with a $2,000 order, may lead one day to $10,000 orders. Some companies require that you have a storefront, a so-called brick-and-mortar shop, before you can be a dealer. Others allow online dealers. You will likely have to get a tax-exempt certificate from your state government, so that you don't have to pay sales tax on the products you buy wholesale. Requirements vary by state, but this is usually a simple application that can be completed very quickly.

Many companies will also advance you a small line of credit to start, perhaps $1,000, and will allow you thirty or sometimes even sixty days to pay. There are thousands of products you can sell, from sporting goods to clothing to books. Starting off small means you may not get a huge volume discount that the larger retailers do, but your overhead will be lower, and you can afford to get lower profit margins since you don't have employees to pay or expensive lease payments to make.

And if all else fails in the search for an idea, there is always another fallback position. As we mentioned in the previous chapter, 93 percent of new businesses are copies of existing businesses. You can simply copy, borrow, or "steal" an idea from someone else. Call it an homage. There is no shame in this. There's always a second player that has copied the first. There's no reason to be ashamed of it. You should go out there and copy someone else's business idea, as there is nothing wrong with it.

A Good Idea Is an Idea Worth Copying

Assume you're at a restaurant, eating with some friends. You say, "I am going to start a business." They respond, "That is so cool! What type of business?" Your response, "Well, I'm actually starting a green, chemical-free landscaping company." They are impressed, excited for you. "Wow, that sounds really cool!" they say. They don't say, "Oh, yeah, I read about that in *Entrepreneur* magazine. You are just copying somebody." Your friends don't say that! They won't care if you are copying someone else's business. You do not lose cool points or street cred for that reason. The coolness comes from starting your own business and being successful. It doesn't come from anything else. What's cool is the fact that you had the fortitude to go out there and do what they're too scared to do. That's where coolness comes from! Will your employees care? Your customers? Your bank account? Nope. There will never be a situation where you find yourself saying, "Yeah, I have one of those bank accounts where they take twenty cents of every dollar because my idea was a copy." Have you heard of that bank account? It doesn't exist.

Many wannabe entrepreneurs wait to find their idea. They wait for a bolt of creativity lightning to strike them. Unfortunately, it is probably not going to happen that way. We have met a thousand people who are waiting to find their idea. They're going to be waiting for a long time. "I'm gonna find it one day," they say, forever waiting for that inspiration. "I'm going to be inspired one day, and all of a sudden, I'm going to have a great new idea." Sorry, but the chances are you probably will not. So, for the 93 percent of us who drew monsters with three heads but learned not to do so later on, let's go find a cool idea, adapt it to our town, and make some money.

The question then becomes "Where should I find ideas to copy?" There is an easy answer to that one. We suggest reading *Inc.* magazine and *Entrepreneur*, or using Google to search for phrases such as "top new business ideas." Check the blogs to find a success story. And to make it even easier, in the Appendix of this book, we list more than two dozen businesses we think you can start in less than three months and for less than $5,000. It's really as simple as looking around, reading your newspaper to see what successful people are doing, and trying to find one idea that sounds like it would be fun.

Keys to Creativity

Even though we have found a way for you to find a business idea, we still want you to work on improving your creativity. After all, although it might not take creativity to launch a new business, it will help you distinguish yourself from some of the other businesses. Creativity is a skill, learned just like any other. If you are a religious person, you need to spend time reading your Bible or Koran. If you are a master chef, you need to spend time tasting spices, watching cooking shows, and reading the recipe books. If you are an entrepreneur, you need to spend time working on your creativity.

We must stress that creativity is a skill just like any other. It must be practiced, and practice leads to improvement. Some men are obsessed with sports, watching ESPN and reading the sports section of the newspaper every day. Some people are obsessed with ice skating and watch every ice-skating event on television. Some people are obsessed with cars or stereos or cuisine and religiously read the appropriate magazines. As we have stated earlier in this book, having a unique idea is not a requirement for successful entrepreneurship. It's perfectly fine to stand on the shoulders of those who've come before you. But coming up with a novel idea can't hurt. You should put time into creativity and treat it like any other hobby. You should talk to your friends about it, read the appropriate sources, devote time to it, and nurture it.

LESSON #9

Creativity isn't an inherited trait, it's a learned skill. Practice and work at your creativity if you want to put it to use in launching your business.

Have you worked on your creativity much since the days of drawing three-headed monsters? Have you done any creativity exercises? Well, get ready, because you're going to start doing some now. It's time now for your first homework assignment. We want you to go on a creativity dinner. When was the last time you went to dinner only to practice your creativity? Probably not recently. Most of us have never done something like that.

What do you do when you go to dinner with your friends? You talk about your kids, about work, about what you're doing in your life, and where you're going on vacation. You never sit there and say, "Let's be creative." So our challenge is to go off with somebody, have dinner, and talk only about creative ideas for a potential new business. It might be with someone you met on LinkedIn, in a small business group, or at an entrepreneurship event, but the important part is finding someone willing to have this kind of a conversation.

You would be surprised at the kind of ideas you're likely to generate when you devote the length of an entire meal to casual talk about potential business ideas. The relaxed setting helps you come up with ideas you might not think of at a desk. If you want to get better at riding a bicycle, what do you do? Ride a bicycle! If you want to get better at French, what do you do? Practice your French. If you want to get better at your creativity, what do you need to do?

Another great way to maximize your ideas is to carry around a notepad and a pen at all times. Put another pad of paper and a pen in your car or wherever you spend time thinking. Many of us are most creative when we are asleep, so you might want to keep a set near the bed as well. A lot of people are creative doing normal, mundane things like cleaning the house, taking a shower, or shaving, when their minds are on something else. You never know when you're going to come up with your next great idea, and if it hits you when you're unprepared for it, you just might forget. Also, being constantly prepared for a great idea makes it much more likely that you'll actually have one.

When you're lying in bed, sleeping, for instance, you may wake up in the middle of the night with an idea and know it's a winner. If you don't write it down right away, you will remember that you had an idea, but you won't remember what the idea was. You'll just want to shoot yourself then, unable to shrug off the thought, "I was going to be a billionaire!" Well, that's probably an exaggeration, but you see what we're getting at.

One of the best things you can do to improve your creativity is to get rid of things that sap your creativity as much as possible. The number one move we can recommend taking in that direction is drastically reducing the amount of television in your life. We love television, so we're not saying to abstain completely. But you are more creative when you learn to get away from it more often.

Spend time on your vacations being creative and looking around for new ideas. You never know what products you are going to see in use overseas that can be replicated elsewhere in the world. Here's an example: In Japan, there is a product called Gatsby. Gatsby are menthol baby wipes that you use when you get hot to wipe your brow and cool off. They sell them at baseball games and places like that—outdoor sporting events. People have never seen anything like this in America, but this is a billion-dollar industry in Japan. So look around, and look at the world around you. Try using some of your vacation time to casually look for new products you can copy at home. Your goal is to find something your country has that a foreign country doesn't have or vice versa. We wish someone sold Gatsby sweat wipes where we live in the United States. They are incredibly refreshing.

Brainstorming

Finally, we would like to introduce some rules for brainstorming. Brainstorming is the primary method by which you will improve your creativity and the process you should use during your creativity dinner. Brainstorming, as you are probably aware, is the process of trying to come up with as many different ideas as possible for a particular topic. For example, you may need to come up with a list of names for a new business. When you brainstorm, creativity is what's important; being practical is not important. It's important to have fun with the thought experiment and let your mind run wild. It's not important that you follow some set process or try to get things exactly right, but there are some rules that are helpful in guiding your brainstorming.

First, each brainstorming session should be designed to answer one particular question, like a name for your new company. You need to have a clear idea of what you want to get out of the session. Second, it's important to remember that there are no wrong or silly ideas. Negativity should not be allowed in the room. At no time will anyone laugh at anyone's suggestion in a mocking way. It's OK to ask "how" in order to prod somebody further, but never as a challenge meant to shoot down someone's idea.

No idea should be instantly dismissed, and that's because ideas are contagious. The crazy idea that your friend Fred just had may inspire your friend Sally to come up with a truly brilliant idea. One person's ideas drive the creativity of the person next to him or her. Pretty soon, you'll generate so many quality ideas that you'll need a list to keep track of them all. You need a dry-erase board or several big pieces of paper or something like that, and make sure every idea gets written down. Look at that list, and see if any of the ideas already written down inspire a new idea. Remember, ideas can come from anywhere. For instance, the list may say, "24-hour day care," but because you are currently having issues with your elderly grandma, you may be inspired to add "adult day care" to the list.

Creativity is not a necessary part of entrepreneurship. It can help, and there are many examples of creative entrepreneurs. But do not let your lack (or your *perceived* lack) of creativity stop you from moving forward. There are lots of ways to get around not having an original idea. God may strike people with creativity lightning bolts, but we do not suggest you wait for it.

4

Bootstrapping Your Business

IN THE ENTREPRENEURIAL COMMUNITY, THERE is a great debate concerning what you should do once you have a business idea. Many entrepreneurial experts recommend writing long, complicated business plans to evaluate every aspect of the venture. Others say a feasibility study is the next critical step.

Certainly, writing a business plan can be extremely useful, and whether you go through with it or not, the process itself is useful. Even the most experienced entrepreneurs must go through the market research, strategic planning, and financial analysis to see if their new idea is in fact a salable one or not.

We believe there is another approach altogether, once you've decided on an idea. To us, the best business plan entails *actually selling product* and letting the market decide whether your goods are wanted, whether your sales pitch is right, and if your price is too high or too low. We are not by any means discounting the value of a business plan. It is a worthy endeavor, and certainly the research must get done, but is there intrinsic value in spending fifty to a hundred hours writing the plan itself? Perhaps that time could be better spent selling the service or product to see what the market is telling you about your price, marketing, support, and sales materials.

LESSON #10

Your goal is to create a product or service that will sell. Let the market validate whether you've created a salable idea by making it available for purchase ASAP.

An Alternative to Long Business Plans

As we've mentioned before, all of the authors of this book have started profitable businesses. Jim and his friend Doug wanted to start their education company, ACE, back in 1993. At the time, neither of them had ever heard of bootstrapping, venture capital, or many of the other terms that entrepreneurs should know. In fact, it is safe to say they knew next to nothing! As it turned out, though, their lack of sophistication and experience could have been one of the reasons their plan was ultimately so successful. Toward the beginning, they did begin to write a five-page business plan, but they stopped writing once they realized that the questions presented in the plan had no immediate or obvious answers.

For example, Jim and Doug were stumped when it came time to predict how the market would respond to their product. They had no idea. So instead of finishing a lengthy, detailed business plan, they simply proceeded to begin executing the plan they'd roughly sketched out. The first step involved securing locations for their educational product. They envisioned teaching children computer skills at prestigious locations around the United States, and after a very short amount of work, they were able to secure two weeks of time during the summer at Stanford University in Palo Alto, California, and at Massachusetts Institute of Technology in Cambridge, Massachusetts. At that point, they had no teachers, curriculum, students, or anything else that might be deemed necessary to run a summer education program for kids.

Consider how much risk was involved in their actions so far. They had invested exactly zero dollars and perhaps five hours of time, mostly spent communicating with the two universities, and maybe ten hours in writing their truncated business plan. We can safely say they had risked nothing. Next, the pair had many choices about what they could do next. They chose to run ads with only basic information about the camp, referring people to a toll-free phone number they could call if they wanted to learn more. They spent about $300 in each market on a small ad that would appear in parenting magazines. The ad offered almost no details or information, but it worked in capturing some attention.

When the parents did call, Jim and Doug let the phone go to voice mail after a brief introductory message. Simply put, the two of them were unable—maybe even a little afraid—to speak with a parent, since they did not know the answers to most of the questions they imagined would be forthcoming. The message simply invited parents to leave their name and address and assured them that a brochure would be forthcoming soon. Of course, no brochure existed. How much risk did their business venture involve now? To put a price on it, they had risked exactly $600 for ads in Cambridge and Palo Alto, a figure that allowed them to test the market and see if there was a demand for their soon-to-be-devised product. It turned out to be a pretty good investment, since they not only determined market interest, but also collected many names of potential customers.

In fact, within two weeks, they collected about a hundred names and addresses, indicating tremendous interest in their educational product. They then spent about two weeks designing a very simple brochure to mail to the parents. As they designed the brochure, they had to make quite a few basic decisions about the eventual product. Price, classes offered, the pickup and drop-off schedule, faculty, food, and countless other factors had to be decided so that the brochure would be all-inclusive. The brochure was printed in two colors, black and red, and still looks good today. Jim and Doug spent about $600 getting one thousand copies printed and another $50 or so on postage, bringing the total investment to roughly $1,250. Two weeks later, their first $100 deposit check arrived—and the pair had a new dilemma.

At this point, Jim and Doug had neither incorporated nor created a checking account. All of the expenses had been paid for using a personal credit card, and there had been no need to legally create the business. They tried to deposit the check, but the bank would not let them open a checking account until the business had been incorporated. Dutifully, they resolved their legal issues, opened bank accounts, and formalized the company. These are all simple procedures and should not deter anyone from launching a business. Almost all of this work, including incorporation, can now be done online at a number of websites, including several that specialize in preparing legal documents, without even leaving your home. And it can be done at a very low cost.

It is critical to remember to reduce risk by not spending money on frivolous, unnecessary items. In this instance, the money went only toward quickly bringing in paying customers. There is an old saying that you don't really have a business until you sell something. (You will become quite familiar with this saying by the end of this book.) Once you have that first check or credit card payment from a customer, you have a bona fide business. A fancy business plan resting comfortably on your computer hard drive is not a business, even if it is written by the smartest MBAs from Harvard. A business plan is theory. Payment from a customer is not only real money in your bank account, but also validation that there is a real demand for the product or service you are offering.

LESSON #11

Legally creating the business with your state and the Internal Revenue Service must be completed around the time the first check arrives. Why incorporate an idea that hasn't been tested or proven?

Bootstrapping vs. Raising Capital

Bootstrapping is a metaphor for improving yourself through your own, unaided efforts. The expression "to pull yourself up by your bootstraps" originated in the early 1800s and referred to a loop or a handle at the top of your boots. You could reach down into the mud and pull yourself out by tugging at your boots. In business, bootstrapping means to make oneself into a success without external help or capital. People who start new businesses through bootstrapping fund their development through internal cash flow and are very conservative with expenses. The main benefit of bootstrapping is that you greatly reduce your risk because you are not beholden to any investors. Since Jim and Doug started off with their own capital, we would certainly say they bootstrapped their business, which grew to earn about $12 million a year in revenue.

The opposite of bootstrapping is raising capital through external means such as outside investors or loans from a bank, family members, or friends. Most aspiring entrepreneurs get stuck on this step. People spend years trying to raise money and use it as the excuse for why they have not started a business. The excuse becomes that they are trying to raise money, and once they raise money, they will test their idea and start the business. But this could take years and does not provide the benefit of knowing whether the idea is any good. Raising funds can be a disease that prevents a business from getting started. Many entrepreneurs make the mistake of spending too much time on raising capital. Our advice is to skip the raising of capital and move directly on to selling product. The way to do this is by investing only money you already have access to. This will greatly reduce your risk, allow for testing your product or service, and get you down the path sooner.

LESSON #12

Low-risk entrepreneurs bootstrap their businesses, starting with very little cash and using creative methods to grow internally.

The major objection to this method we hear from entrepreneurs is this: "My business will take a lot of money to get started." Unfortunately, many times, this worry is all too true. After all, starting a cell phone company or a computer manufacturer can in fact require hundreds of millions of dollars, and when people get ideas about entrepreneurship, they tend to think big. One of Chris's favorite stories is about a man who came to him with the idea of starting a three-level bar, with each floor rotating and featuring a different style of music. The man felt that his gimmick alone would be enough to make the bar successful. Every time Chris raised an objection, the man simply responded, "Yeah, but the bar has three levels!" Chris asked if a rotating dance floor would bring in enough new customers to justify the cost of the electricity and the moving parts. The answer was, of course, the same as always: "The bar has three levels!" The only problem was that in order to make this bar to spec, construction would have cost several million dollars. Our friend Joey Tatum, who runs the bars and restaurants we mentioned earlier, has seen many restaurants come and go, especially the ones that spent way more money than he did on startup costs. These restaurants then must figure out ways to continually make way more money in order to justify the added expense of their startup costs.

If your business plan requires millions of dollars that you do not have to get started, we simply say, "Do not start that business." If you are Bill Gates and want to start a three-level restaurant that spins, we think it's a great idea! The hard truth, though, is that you are not Bill Gates (we think) and therefore should set your goals more realistically. Not everyone gets to start a cell phone company. So we are going to limit our discussions to businesses that can be started for minimal investment.

According to our definition, using your own resources to start a business is what bootstrapping is all about. Remember, our definition refers to internal funds. If you can afford to start the business and not put your entire financial life at risk, we support your goal. Until you reach that point, we would like to show you how to start a business with as little money as possible. The Appendix of this book lists more than two dozen businesses you can start quickly and cheaply without incurring tremendous risk.

Outside Funding

Using the other methods of raising capital (loans, friends and family, outside investors) will require you to spend months or even years on the process of raising capital. Getting a bank loan, for instance, takes on average three to six months, assuming the market is strong. However, in today's market, it can be nearly impossible. Banks are increasingly averse to risk in today's economy. Their business plans work assuming that 97 to 98 percent of the loans are repaid in a timely fashion. Helping you test your market or develop a prototype does not meet that standard.

Getting help from your friends and family is another popular way entrepreneurs raise money. It is also a great way to ensure you never speak to that person again. Doing business with your best friend or with your uncle's money is almost a surefire recipe for disaster. While it may seem like the easy thing to do, we can assure you that in the end, you'll regret your decision and probably lose a friendship.

You can easily spend two to three years chasing venture capital money, and it's a very expensive process. Assume you get an introduction to a venture capitalist and she is interested in meeting you. She will call and tell you that she loves your business plan and wants to hear more. Since your business depends on her firm's funds, you respond that you can be there in two days, and you buy a very high-priced airline ticket. After all that money and time spent, you still might not have any capital to show for the effort. Quickly, you will see that raising venture capital can be very expensive. Why not just spend those two or three years building your business?

Outside funding has consequences. While it may seem as if you have won the lottery, you may in fact be doing your business serious harm by accepting outside capital. Consider instead the value of going to market early and learning how to sell your particular product and what the market response is likely to be. If you raise capital, you will be much less likely to learn from the market, because instead of learning how to sell your product, you were focused on how to sell the idea of your product to investors. One investor will give you advice, which will flavor your next presentation and alter it in a way you think will increase your chances of raising capital. Over time, you are not selling your product but selling an idea that is being shaped not by customers but by investors. You are better off having the market, not some investor, determine the validity of your product.

Also, when you have large sums of money available to start your business, you are more likely to spend the money unwisely. When resources are limited, even extremely limited, you are more likely to spend the money conservatively and only on things that must be purchased. When resources are ample, you are more likely to purchase new computers for all of your employees, hire the most in-demand chief financial officer money can buy, and rent expensive office space.

Jim and Doug bootstrapped their business for the first six years and then made the mistake of raising capital to build a new business line. After spending nearly two years raising the capital, when it came in, they spent money like drunken sailors on fancy new office space and lots of pretty furniture they did not need. They were even shortsighted enough to buy a machine that projected a laser image of their logo dancing on the lobby floor. It was very cool, but did it bring in revenue? No, of course it didn't. Jim and Doug sold the entire business a year later at a profit, but had they wasted less money, the paycheck at the end would have been even larger.

Once you have sold your ideas to investors, especially venture capitalists, they expect you to execute the plan as presented in your business plan. There are even clauses in the contracts you will sign that say if you deviate from the plan, there can be harsh penalties. Your flexibility in responding to changing market conditions will be reduced, and as you finally enter the market, you will have a harder time learning from your customers, because the venture capitalist is the one who is running the show. It is harder to quickly change your business model, based on what customers are telling you, when the guys in the suits, the venture capitalists, are looking over your shoulder. Having money to spend can be a curse and can hide the faults of the plan.

One of the scenarios that frequently fails is that of a successful senior executive who decides to start a business. This executive is used to fancy offices, a secretary, and a whole team of employees. He or she can probably raise money easily, cashing in on strong connections and industry experience. But the executive is used to doing business in a certain way—with a personal secretary to answer phone calls and take dictation, make lunch appointments, and provide other luxuries a bootstrapped business can't afford. Instead of starting small, the executive hires excess staff and soon has a monthly burn rate that quickly challenges the firm's balance sheet. With superfluous spending siphoning cash from the really vital aspects of getting the company off the ground, such as marketing and sales, these companies often run out of money very quickly and collapse.

LESSON #13

Burn rate is the amount of cash flow needed to keep the doors open monthly. Growing burn rates often kill businesses.

Rules of Bootstrapping

Compared with outside funding, bootstrapping is a better way to start a business. It may be slower, less sexy, and counterintuitive, but you are in fact better off growing on internal funds in an organic fashion. You may feel that if you only had more money, you could really grow the business, but that sentiment is frequently wrong.

Bootstrapping is better for the business. It makes you focus on profits and cash flow, and it frees you to spend time on selling instead of raising outside capital, and on solving problems that are truly keeping the company from making a profit, such as low sales volume and excess inventory. Having cash can hide a multitude of mistakes and the long-term problems of the business.

Bootstrapping is better for the owner. It lets you maintain equity and control, learn more, and have an easier time selling the company in the end.

Bootstrapping is better for the employees. They work at a firm where there is a clear and absolute line of authority, and they are taught a surefire way to sell a product. Also, more shares are available for them in employee stock option plans.

Overall, bootstrapping forces you to be more realistic, to not waste time, and to be better prepared for the long run. Hopefully, we have established that bootstrapping is far superior to raising capital. If you're willing to borrow an idea from someone else, as 93 percent of successful entrepreneurs do, and if you remove the thought that you must have capital before you start, there are no legitimate reasons preventing you from being a business owner now.

If you follow our rules for bootstrapping, you should be able to bootstrap your idea and get it up and running within the first ninety days.

Bootstrap Rule #1: Get Operational Quickly

As we've already said, one of the best things you can do to reduce risk is to begin selling immediately. Hopefully you'll generate revenue right from the very beginning. Remember Ben Feldman, the dog-blanket guy? He helped launch an ocean-freight auditing business that would ensure imports were classified correctly. Ben would earn a percentage on any money he saved his client. His first client saved $380,000 because of the audit, and at a take of 25 percent, in his first two weeks of work Ben made close to $100,000.

Bootstrap Rule #2: Look for Quick Sales

If you can find a product that will sell immediately to large numbers of customers, you can actually use those sales to finance your startup, using the sales (known in the business world as receivables) as collateral for a loan. Our intrepid protein importer and exporter, Eric Joiner of AJC International, started his company with a $1,000 investment. But the nature of the business demanded a substantial line of credit so he could purchase items, which he would then ship to other countries. He was able to secure customers for his products and then obtain a $259,000 line of credit and a $750,000 loan collateralized against those receivables. It was an expensive loan in the short term, costing him 51 percent of the business.

In the end, his investors, who put up $510,000, ended up selling their shares back to Eric for just over $2 million. Eric is polite enough to call it a "great deal for both sides," even though his investors made a 300 percent profit in just a year or two. However, in the long term, it was a very profitable loan for Eric. With this line of credit, he expanded into Japan and its pork market, which generated a huge return on investment. Eric says, "Having that loan allowed us to expand and get off to a quick start in a new market."

Bootstrap Rule #3: Offer High-Value Products

Jim and Doug's educational products were the most expensive on the market. When other competitors of the era were charging $300 to $400 per week for computer summer camp, they charged $600 to $900 per week. Many consumers believe that the more expensive the product is, the better it must be, but you have to back this up by providing a better product and better service in exchange for the higher price.

We do not like to compete on price, simply because the only way to be more competitive is to be cheaper or lower your profit margins.

Imagine being in a price war with Walmart, in which case, eventually your profit margins will be close to 1 percent. To bootstrap, you must compete on high performance and after-sales service so that your perceived value, and hence your return on investment, is higher. Always position your company as the best.

Bootstrap Rule #4: Forget the Crack Team of Recruits

Entrepreneurs must realize that in the beginning of their company's life cycle, they must be the chief salesperson, chief marketing officer, chief fulfillment officer, chief financial officer, and the person in charge of cleaning the toilet every day. To bootstrap successfully, entrepreneurs, especially lifers like that senior executive we mentioned earlier, must sacrifice their own vanity and do all of the jobs that previously had been done by a large support team.

Bootstrap Rule #5: Understaff

David Stahl and his software company take this to the extreme. Their company, Infinovate, hires employees only when there is already a signed contract for their services. By constantly remaining understaffed, he is able to keep costs down and in the beginning was able to bootstrap his way to success quickly. His first contract was fulfilled by three people when most companies would have done the work with five.

Bootstrap Rule #6: Keep Growth in Check

It may seem counterintuitive, but slow, steady growth is preferable to fast, explosive growth. The second outcome usually requires a tremendous influx of capital. Growing organically is maybe not as sexy, but it's more likely to produce a company with no debt that is able to weather recessions and crises.

Bootstrap Rule #7: Focus on Cash, Not Profit

While we would never recommend selling a product or performing a service below cost, we certainly believe that profit is not always the most important aspect of your business. At the beginning, when you are just hoping to stay afloat, your worry should not be profit margin, but cash flow. The old expression "Cash is king" is true. Sometimes simply treading water is your best strategic option, and you are better off cutting your profit margin to the bone simply to stay in business. At the very beginning of your business, you will need to do work at cost to facilitate growth. Being able to point to satisfied customers will significantly help your ability to land profitable projects in the future.

At the beginning of your business, it can be difficult to secure a sale, especially in a service-based business. Many times prospects will ask, "How long have you been in business?" or "Who are some of your past customers?" These questions can be very difficult to answer. The best way to finesse the situation is to say something along the lines of this: "You are my first customer. Therefore I know that my business future is contingent on making you so happy that you will tell all of your associates about my services. You are going to get better performance from me because my future is dependent on not only satisfying you, but satisfying you to such a high degree that you tell your friends about me."

Bootstrap Rule #8: Associate with Others' Brand Names

When Jim and Doug started their computer education business, they were twenty-five and twenty-six years old and had absolutely no previous educational experience. Why would any parent send their child to learn from these two? To overcome this problem and establish immediate credibility, they made their first two locations Stanford and MIT. While these universities were not, in fact, endorsing their products, it certainly would seem like the universities were offering their blessings. After all, the universities did allow them to rent space on campus. For a new company, the value of being associated with such great universities cannot be measured. Over time, the duo was able to add sponsorships from Microsoft, Intel, Hewlett-Packard, Swatch, and hundreds of other huge brand names, all of which made the educational product seem even more legitimate and prestigious.

Bootstrap Rule #9: Do Everything In-House

Even when they needed to mail ten thousand brochures, Jim and Doug would address and stamp each letter themselves. They did not have much money, but they did have time and friends. It costs perhaps five cents to have an outsourcing company attach postage to each envelope for you, which would have cost them $500 for the whole mailing. Instead, they would order a few pizzas and invite their parents, girlfriends, and friends to come over for a night of free pizza and stamp licking.

Bootstrap Rule #10: Do Sales Yourself

An entrepreneur must be able to sell, especially his or her own product or service. No one will sell the product as well as the originator. After hiring salespeople, the entrepreneur should be in charge of all sales education, because he or she should by definition be the best salesperson in the office. Remember that startups are based on selling products, and the entrepreneur must develop the skills necessary to achieve sales.

Bootstrap Rule #11: Start in Your House or Garage

The idea of starting a business in your home or garage is truly a cliché at this point. We have all heard how Michael Dell started his company in a dorm room and how Apple Computer was started in a garage. Even though this kind of startup method is a cliché, it is great advice. Office space is a luxury you cannot afford. One of the biggest mistakes that two- or three-year-old businesses make is to upgrade their offices. Jim and Doug went from 1,200 square feet of office space costing $500 a month to 8,000 square feet of office space that cost tens of thousands of dollars a month. It took them two years to recover from this fiasco.

Bootstrap Rule #12: Don't Pay Yourself or Others

Just as you are not going to waste money on logos and shirts, you can rarely afford to pay yourself at the beginning as well. One of the reasons we espouse low-risk entrepreneurship is that young businesses can rarely afford to throw off money to the owner. There is simply not enough profit in the beginning to pay yourself a living wage. Our recommendation is to start a business on the side that requires your time in the morning or evening before or after your normal job. In year one, let's hope you make $10,000 in sales. In year two, go for $100,000 in sales and $15,000 in profit. And in year three, let's hope you can afford to pay yourself $50,000 from the $300,000 of sales that you have. This slow-growth plan reduces your risk and makes sure that you have active health insurance the entire time.

Bootstrap Rule #13: Argue Every Price

Prices are meant to be negotiated. If you go to Asia or Europe, there is a strong culture for haggling and negotiating prices; in fact, you lose credibility if you do not negotiate the price of underwear bought from a stall in a flea market or the price of software designed for your company. Negotiate every price. Tell the people you are buying goods and services from that you are broke and a new company and in need of a special "new-company discount." The very worst that can happen is that they laugh at you and deny your request. Ask again even after they laugh at you, and tell them you are serious. Saving money at every step of the game could make the difference between having a profitable company or an unprofitable one.

Bootstrap Rule #14: Harness Word-of-Mouth Advertising

Advertising can be a major expense for your new company, but you can cut those costs to near zero through blogging and social network sites such as Twitter and by building e-mail lists. We know one entrepreneur who is followed on Twitter by thousands of people and has an e-mail marketing list in the tens of thousands. She has yet to spend any money on advertising. All of her marketing is done through word of mouth, which has the added benefit of being much more credible than traditional marketing.

Bootstrap Rule #15: Use the Royal *We*

Entrepreneurs should always speak in the plural. Do not say, "I will get it done." Say, "We will get that done." While it makes a small difference, it still might make a big enough difference to be useful. Never lie, but try to leave the impression that your firm is already established, which will give customers more confidence that you can and will get the job done. Don't announce your start date if it was only a year ago, and do whatever you can to make it seem older than it is. For example, you can blog for months before the site goes live, so that a new customer will see a longer history.

Bootstrap Rule #16: Use Free Labor

Use as much free labor as you can get. Interns are a great source of free capital. Many states offer government-paid internship positions, and college kids are willing to work for free if the job looks good on their résumé. Call a business professor, or look on Facebook for a local entrepreneur club, and offer students the opportunity to be part of a startup. Many will jump at the chance. When Jim and Doug started their kids' educational company, Jim made his mother come along as a nurse, to give them more credibility. Her major nursing function was to hand out Ritalin, but just having her there made the young entrepreneurs seem more legit to the parents.

Bootstrap Rule #17: Look for Import/Export Opportunities

Cherie Stine, our rubber band bracelet entrepreneur, demonstrated this point. Her firm was only two months old when it started importing from China, getting a more reliable supplier with better support, and reducing costs. Imagine finding a product that you can import or export. Many websites list buyers or sellers that are looking for a U.S. partner. For example, the Japanese government runs an organization called the Japan External Trade Organization, which has a website (http://www.jetro.org) that lists Japanese firms interested in importing U.S. goods. Scan the list, find a need you can fulfill, find a supplier, and become an intermediary. If you use other resources, like UPS's Capital Group, you can easily structure the deal so you have almost no risk. This is what Cherie did. She identified a demand in the United States, found a Chinese supplier, and is projected to sell $7 million worth of her product.

Bootstrap Rule #18: Get Advances from Customers

Are customers willing to paying advances? Sure, they are. They are called deposits, and you can ask for them for almost any product or service. Or if you are opening a restaurant, sell a "permanent table" to an investor. Whenever such customers come in, they get to dine at that table, and dinner is free.

Bootstrap Rule #19: Let Customers Fund Your Research

Cherie Stine was a great example of this rule. Before selling her rubber band bracelets, she got the idea from watching what her kids liked. She let her eventual customers tell her what was in demand. Now that she is up and running and successful, she studies sales patterns to see what to order and what is going to be hot next. Listen to your customers. If clients come in asking for a particular version of something you don't have, order it. They are telling you what will be hot next.

Bootstrap Rule #20: Forecast from the Bottom Up

Decide in advance how much you want to make during the first year of your business. Assume you want to make $50,000 in profits and that from each sale you make $1,000 profit. Clearly then, you need to make fifty sales during the year, or about one a week. Forecasting from the bottom up gives you the ability to meet your sales goals and therefore to control your startup costs and growth rate. You know, for example, that for every four customers you meet, you sell one unit. This means you must meet with four customers every week. To generate four customers, you must make one hundred telephone calls to get the appointments. Using this method, you can back into your sales and profit necessity by calculating the number of calls you must make or advertisements you must place. If making one hundred calls in a week is impossible, at least you will know and be able to work backward from that point.

Bootstrap Rule #21: Ship First, Then Test

Get the product after shipping, and then test it. We are stealing this idea from Guy Kawasaki, the famous Apple executive and now venture capitalist. He says speed to market is the most important asset you can develop, so technology companies in particular often will ship a product and let the customers do the testing while the bugs and kinks are worked out of the system.

Bootstrap Rule #22: Service Businesses Are Easier

Finally, let's realize that in America, service businesses are much easier to bootstrap than product-based businesses. Most of the entrepreneurs in this book are service-based entrepreneurs, and that is understandable, since about 80 percent of the U.S. economy is now services based. Also, it is nearly impossible to compete with China's ability to manufacture goods at considerably cheaper prices than in America. The advantage of a service-based business is that there is no inventory to purchase in the beginning. Since you are providing the work that produces the service, up-front investment is much lower, and it is easier to start. The rest of the world is somewhere between 10 and 30 percent services based, so the possibility of exporting your service business also is very high.

Bootstrap Rule #23: You Don't Need a Business Plan

A common misconception is that an entrepreneur must start by writing a detailed business plan. The low-risk entrepreneur doesn't need that. The bootstrapping entrepreneur starts small, with one or two sales, slowly building with little if any debt and using his or her day job as a cushion, creating a sustainable, profitable business from day one. Using this formula, the only person who would read your business plan is you, and you already know what the plan is. Planning is important; spending weeks writing about it is not important. Later in your career as an entrepreneur, a business plan may be a good idea as you venture into larger companies and indeed want to use someone else's money to do so. But for now, that's not necessary. Spend that time selling.

More than anything, remember that the details of a business are less important than simply getting your business off the ground. Nothing matters but getting that first paying customer, and then another and another. Every sale builds on itself. In the long term, what matters is not the fancy office or title. It's the profit that you will use to pay your bills, grow the business even larger, and secure the self-made future you always wanted.

5

The Power of International Trade

MANY PEOPLE SEE INTERNATIONAL ENTREPRENEURSHIP—starting a business that involves importing and exporting—as inherently more difficult than starting a domestic business. Just the idea scares some people. Of course, there are perhaps more considerations when doing business internationally, but ultimately, doing so can be one of the best ways to start a business with very low risk.

It may seem counterintuitive, but international business can have less risk than domestic business. As we will show in this chapter, many businesses benefit greatly from global exposure, and even though it may seem daunting at first, we highly recommend that you consider international business from the very beginning. In fact, your company could sell exclusively overseas from day one.

Paths to an International Business

There are several basic paths to growing a successful international business. The most common method would be gradually evolving the business over time into international sales. Most businesses fit into this category. They first become successfully engaged in domestic business, and then out of the blue, a client calls and asks if the company can supply its product or service to Mexico or France. Other businesses are born international, starting as an international enterprise from the very beginning. Our friend Eric Joiner's chicken brokerage would fit into this category.

Whichever path you take, starting an international business might involve less risk than launching a domestic one, and the international approach can be a great way to bootstrap a business.

Fears About Starting an International Business

The fear of the unknown is what makes international business appear difficult. First, languages and cultures are often dramatically different. You may not understand how to do business in a certain culture or how to communicate with potential business partners in a foreign market. In fact, you may not know how to get in touch with or establish relationships with people overseas. When no connections are already in place, it may seem virtually impossible to find a partner who will protect your interests and help you grow your business. As you will see later in this chapter, that worry is unfounded. Finding overseas partners is, in fact, very easy.

You may think that any business you might start would be too small to go international or that you cannot compete overseas with the big boys. After all, many of the companies that do business overseas are so firmly established that they leave no room for competition, right? Wrong. The global market is so large that no one company can monopolize it. Remember the furniture business Jim started with his students, importing chairs from Pakistan? He managed to turn a handsome profit from it in only a few months.

Finally, many people are afraid of international financial transactions because they believe getting paid internationally will be riskier and more difficult. The currency will have to be converted, and it will be tricky to figure out what rates to apply for the same products in a different country. This, too, is an unfounded fear. There is a global financial system in place that makes it easy and safe to handle international transactions. Access to these international tools are often no farther away than your nearest bank branch. You will see that international business not only is safe, but also can be a huge bonus for you financially.

Getting Started: Do Something

Of all of the things that must be done to start an international operation, the very first step is the hardest one: springing into action. This is especially true in the age of the Internet, where your Web presence can be seen all around the world. An international customer may discover your website or hear about your product from someone in your local market area and contact you about buying your product or service for the customer's home market. Many businesses that sell internationally developed their overseas market through happenstance. They were not planning to do business overseas, but one day they received that e-mail or telephone call from some unknown person who went on to become their first overseas customer.

Getting this e-mail might come as quite a surprise if you have done nothing to promote to that market and don't know the person contacting you. You may even be inclined to brush off the inquiry, since the person contacting you may not speak English well or did not contact you in a familiar way. But you must pursue this opportunity. With the economy today, you cannot afford to miss any opportunity for growth, even if it is international growth.

If you haven't been contacted yet, there is no reason to wait before getting started on the international level. As discussed in the previous chapter, the first thing you need is a product to distribute. If you have no idea what you want to do, it is a little trickier to know where to start. Instead of asking yourself what you want to export, ask yourself, "What does my state have an overabundance of in stock?" Or ask yourself, "What does my home country have that Japan doesn't?" Get online and search websites for organizations like the Japan External Trade Organization (http://www.jetro.org), the Japanese government agency offering information on products that you can export to Japan, along with tons of advice on how to do it. There are plenty of other sites that can offer similar information for other countries.

A literally endless supply of information about foreign markets is available for free to anyone with a computer. Websites for the U.S. Department of Commerce, your local state export office, Export .gov, International Entrepreneurship, and tons of others will provide you with everything you need to get started. This free information will tell you which markets are best for which products and how to approach a particular market you are interested in. You can easily learn how to do business in a different country and what local rules or regulations you must adhere to in any country in the world. Also, if you are worried about shipping problems, the UPS website has sections for every country in the world. When you enter information about your product, these websites will display all relevant regulations you should know about before doing business in that country.

Many Americans may be concerned that overseas customers may not be interested in their product or service. Just the opposite is true, however. Consumers around most of the world consider American products to be luxurious and desirable. Items that Americans take for granted and do not consider special are highly sought after overseas. For example, Levi's blue jeans are still a very desirable item in Russia and the former Soviet countries, as well as other parts of the world, including Africa. If you look around for them, niches are plentiful. Lingerie is in high demand in Uruguay and Paraguay and is hard to get. You do not need to be a big player to be very successful in overseas markets. Products that are of high quality sell anywhere.

Cultural Issues

Many cultural issues are involved in starting an international business, and you should become familiar with these as you get started. If you are worried about making some kind of faux pas in dealing with a country you've never visited, then you are on the right track—a lot of considerations arise when you go international. With a little bit of research, though, you can assure that your product will be greeted with open arms.

For example, when considering your product and its packaging, you will have to give thought to the meanings of certain colors in various countries. It is an American perception that black is the color of death, but many other countries consider white to represent death. You must consider the color issue when making decisions about your product for international sales. Choosing the wrong color might be off-putting to your potential customers.

You will also need to learn business customs in each market in which you decide to sell your product. In Saudi Arabia and much of Asia, it is expected that you will spend a considerable amount of time getting to know people before you engage in business discussions. Americans are very used to doing business with people they have never met, even conducting business over the telephone and having a relationship that is entirely focused on business. However, in most other countries of the world, businesspeople count on developing some level of personal relationship before beginning negotiations.

Exporting a Service

Compared with tangible goods, services are even better contenders for expansion outside of the United States. As we've pointed out before, about 80 percent of the U.S. economy is now service oriented, meaning we have many service-based companies that have proven that their product is well received by the marketplace. In a country where the service economy is not well developed, these service-based opportunities, ranging from product design to architecture, are ripe for partnering. Find a small local business outside the United States, and partner with it to deliver a service to an overseas market. If the American consumer is willing to pay for a service, it is very likely that customers elsewhere will be interested in paying for that same service too. These types of businesses are cheap and quick to start.

LESSON #14

If you wish to start a business exporting a service overseas, the way to start is to find a partner who lives in the area you wish to service, who will act on-site.

One of the authors of this book, Chris Hanks, owns a coffee shop. After buying beans from the same local supplier for several years, Chris casually asked the supplier about his family and where he got his coffee. As it turned out, the supplier's wife was Vietnamese, and he imported his coffee from Vietnam. After they'd been talking for a while, the supplier opened up and started telling Chris all about the supply needs of Vietnam, one of the world's fastest-growing economies. According to the coffee supplier, Vietnam needed all kinds of things: medical supplies, computers, trucks—basically anything you could think of. What kind of trucks did they need? The heavy-duty trucks commonly seen on the interstate highways, hauling giant trailers full of goods.

We don't talk much theory in this book, mostly opting for practical tips for success. But this is a good example of an academic theory called the corridor principle, which says once you get started and head down the entrepreneurship path, new doors will open as you make your way. As you proceed further, you will be able to see into doors that your previous angle prevented you from seeing. Each door that opens and each room that you see into is a new business opportunity, one that would not have been available had you not started down the hall. Had Chris not been involved with the coffee shop, for instance, he would never have learned about the truck business.

LESSON #15

The corridor principle says doors open only as you walk down the path of opportunity.

Each new opportunity represents a new revenue stream. The more revenue streams you have, the safer you are. How many revenue streams does the average Fortune 100 employee have? One. How many revenue streams does a landscaper with one hundred clients have? One hundred. For this very reason, the landscaper may have a safer financial future. If you are already in business, going international adds revenue streams by adding opportunities for more and more revenue streams. For Chris, adding truck sales to his income mix made his family more secure, not less.

Thus, a new business was born, with Chris and his coffee supplier soon buying used trucks in the United States—on eBay and from truck brokers—and shipping them to Vietnam. It was an international business from day one. The coffee seller's wife, who speaks fluent Vietnamese, located a truck broker in Ho Chi Minh City. They would e-mail the truck broker pictures and specs on trucks for sale in the United States, many of them with as many as 750,000 miles accrued on the diesel engines, but still with a lot of life left in them.

When the broker in Vietnam saw a truck he thought he could resell at a profit, he would buy it from Chris and his partner, paying them a $2,500 fee on each truck. The broker was making all the buying decisions. Chris and his partner were making money simply by finding suitable trucks and shipping them, not a very high-risk endeavor. The trucks had already been preapproved for sale before they were purchased.

Chris and his partner rented a cheap warehouse in Atlanta for around $1,000 a month. The warehouse was a dump but served its purpose. They hired a warehouse manager and started shipping trucks, using day laborers at $10 an hour to break down the vehicles, removing the tires and otherwise compacting them so that two would fit into one shipping container for the six-week slow boat to Vietnam. The warehouse manager handled the customs forms and all the other paperwork as well.

After receiving the trucks, the broker in Vietnam would wire payment through his bank. Before shipping the trucks, Chris and his partner would take out a letter of credit through their bank as an insurance policy in case the payment from Vietnam never arrived. For a small percentage of the value of the trucks, the U.S. bank would guarantee payment as long as the trucks were properly shipped. There was virtually no risk of not getting paid, and in fact, since banks guarantee letters of credit, risk may be even less than in domestic sales.

LESSON #16

The letter of credit is a promise from your bank that if you ship the product correctly, your bank guarantees the payment, even if the overseas buyer never pays. It is a great risk reducer.

Soon, Chris and his partner were shipping eight to ten trucks a month. In the first year alone, the business produced a healthy profit. Chris never set foot in Vietnam and took almost no risk. The business started quickly and required no skills. The trick was making the connection from what his coffee supplier explained to the possibility of actually starting a business. After that, the introduction fell in place from the man's Vietnamese wife to the local Vietnamese broker. But had that not happened, the U.S. Commercial Service would have found a similar opportunity. There are lots of ways to get connected to a broker, such as e-mailing the broker directly and asking to do business with him or her.

This is a strong example of how overseas markets can be lucrative for anyone who wants to take control of his or her future, quickly and cheaply, with no special skills.

International trade actually lowers risk by expanding your customer base. If there is a downturn in the U.S. truck market and you sell used trucks only domestically, your business is more likely to fail. But if you sell worldwide, your risk is reduced. Once you start selling in a country like Vietnam, you will learn of other products needed by consumers there. You start selling trucks and then expand to truck parts. Then maybe it's medical supplies. You learn also about products in Vietnam that may be good for importing into the United States. The opportunities are endless.

Dealing with a Small Player

Currently, less than 1 percent of the 30 million companies in the United States export, which is significantly lower than in other developed countries, according to U.S. Commerce Secretary Gary Locke. More than half (58 percent) of U.S. companies that export do so to only one country. While it is clear from these Commerce Department statistics that many companies are intimidated by doing business abroad, it is easy and profitable.

The fear of the unknown is what makes international business appear difficult. You might think it's virtually impossible to find a partner overseas that will protect your interests and help you grow your business. It very well may be impossible to get a deal with a big foreign company. Adapting as we do, then, it is important to get a deal going with a small player.

In the summer of 2003, Jim Beach went with a group of Georgia State University students to Brazil and Argentina on a study trip abroad. He was excited about the trip for many reasons, but one of them had nothing at all to do with education: he had purchased some quality leather jackets in South Korea years earlier, and these needed replacing. So on the trip to Argentina, Jim was looking forward to the opportunity to buy some new leather.

Argentina, with its vast plains, is known for its beef and leather industries. The capital, Buenos Aires, is known as the Paris of South America and is one of the most fashionable cities in the world. On this trip, Jim discovered many great stores for all types of leather goods. In particular, he was impressed with the capybara leather items in many stores. He'd seen this leather before in American stores, but those items had cost several thousand dollars each—significantly out of his price range. The capybara is like a small pig with porcupine needles on its skin. The leather of this animal is known for being very distressed, soft, and buttery. The animal is considered a pest on the level of a rat, and it's one of the least cuddly animals you would ever find anywhere in the world. It may be very ugly, but the capybara's leather is some of the nicest in the world.

So while Jim was in Buenos Aires, he did quite a bit of shopping, both for himself and for family members back home. He bought about $300 worth of clothes that in the States probably would have cost $1,000. School started very soon after this trip, and Jim was still talking about the clothes during the first weeks of class. The students had heard rumors of Timeless Chair, the company selling chairs made in Pakistan, described in Chapter 1, and they pressed for an in-class startup of their own. After seeing the quality of Jim's jackets, the students believed a leather company importing from Argentina seemed like a natural fit (pardon the pun). Overseas trips should be shopping trips, yes, but they should also be trips on which you shop for ideas, looking for companies and products that can be sold back home.

Members of the class decided to name the company SkinLeather .com, primarily because that URL was available. They started doing research on the Internet, first finding out everything they needed to learn about the culture. They soon discovered the major differences between the Pakistani and Argentine startup experiences. Despite all of its recent economic problems, Argentina has a well-developed system of government agencies, trade shows, and other pieces of the economic engine that Americans would consider familiar. One of the first things the class discovered was that many websites were dedicated to Argentine leather. Many of these were already selling leather to the United States, but most were wholesalers, rather than retailers.

Then the class found a government website named Cuerocima .com.ar. The word *cuero* is Spanish for leather. CIMA is a government-based manufacturers association for the producers of leather in Argentina. This excellent website appears in both English and Spanish. More important, it lists all of the major manufacturers of leather goods in Argentina with telephone numbers, fax numbers, websites, and products of specialty.

The organization also organizes quarterly trade shows, and at the time, one was coming up within the next month. The class had gotten incredibly lucky with good timing, so Jim immediately booked reservations to go back to Argentina for this trade show. The trade show was almost identical to any you would find in the United States, with rows and rows of booths staffed by company salespersons displaying their products. The only difference at all was that everyone was speaking Spanish.

Before leaving for Buenos Aires, Jim made several appointments with government officials and some of the more promising vendors from the government index website, Cuerocima.com.ar. The government officials who were in charge of promoting the leather industry were extremely helpful and willing to introduce Jim to people and to help with any red tape or shipping issues the class might encounter.

Jim already had decided that the products the class would sell would include leather luggage, jackets, purses, and other accessories. But he needed to find out the prices and general terms at which he could expect to secure these, so he asked many different vendors about their policies and prices. After the five days of the show were over, he flew back to Atlanta to select the product and pricing mixes.

The women in the class proved to be more sophisticated shoppers than Jim, so they selected most of the items the class would be selling. Very quickly, they decided on a product mix and were ready to place an order. They e-mailed their orders, getting confirmation within a matter of hours. In the end, they wound up using four different sources: one for exotic leather jackets (lambskin and capybara), one for handbags, one for luggage, and another for leather jackets. From the first company, Jim bought twenty-five purses at an average price of about $15, for a grand total of about $400. For such a small amount of money, Jim was willing to simply pay with a credit card, making the financial piece of the transaction very easy. He had the goods shipped airfreight on American Airlines, arriving in twenty-four hours.

The class had already started building the website before Jim's trip to Buenos Aires. The website would be built on the exact same template as the site for the chair company. The pictures the suppliers were able to provide were of very poor quality and were not usable for the website, so the class started taking pictures in Jim's living room, using a mannequin he purchased from a retail supply store and a black sheet as background. Each item was placed in front of the black sheet, and students took several high-definition pictures. They cropped out all of the black and put the pictures on a white background using Photoshop. It probably took thirty minutes for each item, and well over a hundred different items were initially available on the website. It went live on November 8.

Marketing was the next challenge. Unlike the furniture company, this business would need to be marketed directly to consumers. The furniture company had been marketing only to a very select group of buyers: interior decorators. In contrast, the leather firm needed a unique marketing plan, a wider strategy to let millions of people know that the site existed. Also, because the students were aiming to get the site launched before the end of the semester, they had to build clientele quickly, rather than waiting for the website to appear high in the Google rankings organically. The solution was GoogleAds—the advertising you see on the right side and at the very top of a Google search results page. Google advertising is a big part of how the company makes its billions of dollars every year, as ads can be very expensive. These ads are sold more or less on an auction basis: the more people who want to appear in the number one position for any given search, the higher the price. Whoever is willing to pay the most appears first, so the more general the words you are advertising for, the more expensive the ad will be.

To advertise alongside the search results for "leather jackets" is very expensive (perhaps four or five dollars each time a customer clicks on your website), but to advertise for "lambskin leather jackets" was not nearly as expensive, since not many people will specify those exact keywords. Using more specific keywords reduced the costs and targeted better customers. Another advantage of using Google ads is that you can turn them on and off whenever you want. You can set a $100 advertising budget per day, and as soon as you spend $100, your advertising stops for that day. The class made a list of keywords that would appeal to customers and started advertising in the middle of November. At this point, it was a simple matter of turning the ads on or off depending on the budget. This allows you to tweak both the website and the ads you are running, because you can tell after each day whether the ads are successful. In the end, the Google ads—the only advertising the class used—ended up costing about 8 percent of revenue, which for a brand-new company is pretty cheap.

LESSON #17

When selecting keywords for GoogleAds, be sure to specify as much as possible to get the cheapest ads that will reach the most highly targeted audience.

The total investment for this endeavor was about $3,000 for the trip to Argentina, about $2,500 for the first set of merchandise, about $100 for a mannequin used for photographs, and $100 to set up the company, for a total of about $5,700. At that level of investment, the class needed to sell about fifty coats and twenty handbags or some similar combination to be in the black. With classes ending in mid-December, the students had plenty of time to cover such a small initial investment. Luckily, it was the Christmas season, so potential buyers flocked to the website. The only significant problem the class encountered was that one of the reorder shipments, sent by air, was broken into and partially stolen. The cardboard box was cut along the side with an X-Acto knife, and about half of the box's contents were taken out of the side of the box. Unfortunately, the airline insured by weight, not by the value of the products, and several hundred dollars were lost on that shipment. But the company still made a profit in just one college semester.

Jim and the other members of the class ran the business only a short time before liquidating the merchandise on eBay. Just as with the Timeless Chair company, this classroom example illustrates that the lessons in this book are not theory. Everything we are teaching is so easy to put into action that it can be accomplished in a college classroom in ninety days or less, with a very low-risk investment of only $5,700. Here, Jim once again illustrated the great potential of international trade by importing niche products from overseas and using the Internet to help buy and sell. It can be accomplished in the classroom or in your garage. The world is your marketplace.

Finding Success Overseas

For the ultimate example of a business born to be international, you need look no further than Furniture Origins, a company founded in 2002 by Seth Jutan. Seth is what you might call an overachiever. During high school, he ran little businesses on the side, including a lawn maintenance company that had sixty clients a week before Seth even had a driver's license.

In the process of conducting an academic project during college, Seth decided to start a business selling farming equipment. Soon he made a deal with Bauer, an equipment manufacturer, to sell its heavy machinery and agriculture equipment to people or countries with little money. Seth proposed that if the machinery was purchased with a loan, the buyers could use the machine to generate profits to repay the loan. Bauer countered with a deal one notch better. If Seth could get a country to guarantee a loan, he could arrange financing for the equipment through Austria's EXIM bank. Seth's joint venture with Bauer started with a loan of $5 million. While he was still in college, his project had become a real business.

He later started a company that ran training centers for overseas employees of call centers who would perform order fulfillment over the telephone. He quickly raised $13 million from venture capitalists, grew to six hundred employees in eight offices, and in 2001 sold his interest to other shareholders, who later sold the company to VeriSign. He retired at age thirty-two. It was a happy ending to the entrepreneurial story, but Seth became bored immediately. One day he called his stockbroker, and after getting no reply at the office and calling back several times, Seth called his broker's home number, since the two also knew each other socially. It turned out that the broker had been fired and was now selling furniture on eBay; importing antique reproductions by the container turned $25,000 into $65,000. After finding out that Seth had free time and was bored, and knowing that Seth had lots of international-business experience, the broker asked Seth help out in the furniture business. Seth's first assignment was to go to Indonesia to see if he could bargain for lower prices from suppliers. Seth met the suppliers and in the end bought containers full of furniture for $5,000, paid shipping of $5,000, and sold it to his ex-stockbroker for $17,000 (saving him $8,000). That meant Seth kept a $7,000 profit.

The experience inspired Seth to launch his own wholesale international furniture business, Furniture Origins. Much as Chris's coffee shop led him to selling trucks in Vietnam, Seth had also taken the corridor principle down a new road in international business, of which there are many. Furniture Origins now has offices in eighteen countries. Seth discovered, as many entrepreneurs have, that international trade provides a virtually limitless market. It is a market too massive and too lucrative for an entrepreneur to ignore.

Other entrepreneurs we've mentioned so far have important international components, too. Jeff Galloway travels and teaches running at clinics around the world. Ben Feldman and Terri Alpert import merchandise from around the globe for sale in the United States. Eric Joiner and his trade company always pay on domestic terms, which requires them to offer great customer service for foreign buyers, including a staff that speaks twenty-nine languages and does business in 140 countries.

Cherie Stine, our rubber band bracelet friend, outgrew her supplier quickly, and she was unable to get product fast enough to meet demand for her trendy product. In response, she got on Alibaba .com, sent several e-mails to manufacturers she found on the site, and within three days had placed an order with the only company offering exact duplicates of competing products. Cherie intuitively trusted this one supplier and had a prototype sent from Xiamen. Her suppliers in China allowed her to sell $7 million in the first year.

What do all of these stories have in common? They all feature entrepreneurs who had little or no experience dealing with buyers or sellers on an international level, yet they were able to do so successfully anyway. Don't be afraid to think about selling overseas from the beginning if you want to turn a profit on your business quickly.

6

The Internet: An Entrepreneur's Powerful Global Tool

ANY BOOK THAT DEALS WITH twenty-first century entrepreneurship must discuss the Internet at length. Since our focus on small-investment, low-risk entrepreneurship lends itself to starting an Internet business, this discussion is an absolute necessity. When you know the best ways to work it, the Internet allows you to start a business very quickly—certainly under our ninety-day goal.

The number of small businesses that have been able to carve a niche in online sales is endless. In the world of online sales, inventory accumulation becomes less relevant, and startup costs can be very low. Whether the product is crocheting advice, spice racks, or sex toys, fortunes are being made every day by average people who have learned how to build a following of consumers. And if you ask around, you will find that most of them started out with very little capital.

Henry's Story

Henry Chang is twenty-three years old. During his junior and senior years of college, you couldn't find a student more eager to learn. Some professors actually had to ask Henry to hold his questions, because he too frequently interrupted the professor with a seemingly endless barrage of inquiries. The questions were always good, though—never off topic, and always indicating total attention. However, Henry was usually surfing the Net during class, always ready to dispute any professorial claim that could potentially be refuted by any website.

Henry started an Internet business that generated over $100,000 in profit in under a year, all while going to school full-time. The business was focused on selling consumers older technology that big-box retailers were discontinuing. The way he got his start was by driving all over the South, sometimes for two or three hours at a time, to find retailers that were still selling these discontinued items. He would buy a stash of cameras and disk drives that one particular location of Best Buy would no longer be selling, knowing full well that plenty of potential buyers would be out there.

Henry knew the average sales price, wholesale price, profit margin, and spread of just about every piece of technology on the market. He would sell the merchandise on his own website, eBay, and other online auction websites. His first sale came a week after he started, and he ended up profiting with each transaction. Everything he bought was hugely discounted, and his purchases were very small at first, usually under $1,000, so his risk was incredibly low.

LESSON #18

You must be an expert at something to succeed on the Internet, and your site must demonstrate that expertise explicitly.

There are several lessons to be learned from Henry. He started a business in a field he had extensive knowledge of, which is important, because if you don't know what you're talking about in a field like technology, your potential customers might see right through you. Henry loves tech hardware and would be active in this space even if not running a business. The startup costs were very low, and that allowed for profits to pour in almost immediately. The Net played a critical role is his success, too. It allowed him to buy his merchandise locally and sell it globally. Tapping into huge audiences through eBay and other giant websites meant he could usually sell his products very quickly, which provided a steady cash flow and reduced the need for amassing a huge inventory.

A Sticky Website

Although websites such as eBay are great selling tools, it also helps to have a strong site of your own. A great website must be sticky, meaning users want to spend lots of time on the site, even if they are not purchasing anything. There should be content that draws in customers, even on days they do not plan on buying anything.

We worked with one entrepreneur who had created a social networking site for enthusiasts of extreme sports. The site was getting great traffic and had over thirty thousand active users pretty quickly. Users posted videos of themselves skydiving, white-water rafting, and participating in other adventurous activities. When we came in to talk with the site's owner, we immediately recommended building an online store to monetize the traffic the business was already getting.

Another client had the opposite problem. This client's site included an online store but was not getting enough traffic. We saw adding content to the site as the solution. We helped the client add blogs, informational help sections, and other content to give users a reason to visit more frequently. Sales quickly doubled, as more and more people visited the site to read the content and, while there, saw products they wanted to buy.

LESSON #19

A great website has sections that educate or entertain and a separate section for sales.

Erik's Story

Erik Rostad started playing the violin on his third birthday. He studied the violin, piano, trumpet, guitar, bagpipes, and the Irish uilleann pipes while growing up. In the same time period, Erik also participated in fourteen different sports, counting baseball and track as his favorites. After graduating from the University of Georgia with a bachelor's degree in international business, he landed his first job at Russell Corporation, maker of Russell Athletic apparel. There Erik worked in a small division that was responsible for all aspects of the international sales process, from sales, to production, to the logistics of getting the product from point A to point B. Erik traveled to Latin America over twenty times during his four and a half years at Russell, spending time on both the retail and production floors.

An added benefit of the Russell job was a buildup of frequent-flier miles. Erik used these for personal travel to many spots around Europe, one time flying to Vienna just to catch his favorite opera. The Latin American and European trips further broadened Erik's desire to see more of the world. Toward the end of Erik's time at Russell, he began pursuing a master's degree in international business and soon met two of this book's authors, Jim and Chris. While most college courses taught how to conduct oneself in a corporate setting, Jim and Chris's courses taught students to think for themselves while starting their own business. Up until this point, Erik had never considered starting his own company.

As a final requirement for his degree, Erik took a job in Lima, Peru, for a four-month work-abroad experience. This particular job was twofold. Half of his time was to be spent working for a company that imported heavy machinery from around the world. Erik assisted in building relationships with suppliers from the United States during those four months. The other half of his time was spent starting a new business. Erik decided to develop a website to sell traditional Peruvian products to buyers in the United States. Even though his only website design skills came from a one-hour lecture during a class during graduate school, Erik sat down with a website design manual and soon learned to build basic sites. Within a few weeks, a site was ready. He e-mailed and called suppliers and established wholesale accounts so he could begin selling their products on his site.

Although sales from this venture were small, Erik learned some incredibly valuable lessons. The biggest lesson was website design. Website design is not as hard as many people fear. Designers charge exorbitant prices, because their clients do not know what Web services should cost. We recommend that you go on eBay and buy a DVD set on basic Web skills (start by searching for a "Dreamweaver DVD"; Dreamweaver is the software commonly used to build websites). Spend the weekend watching the series, and you will learn enough to save thousands of dollars. An entrepreneur should be able to make basic changes to his or her own site without the aid of a designer, and should be able to know when a designer is lying about costs.

Erik did exactly this, and upon his return to the United States, friends and contacts from graduate school began asking him to do website design work. He helped them, and after a while, he decided to turn his skills into a company, starting EPR Creations in May 2008. Initial clients were secured by word of mouth and small ads on Craigslist, and these led to more lucrative clients later on. With the miraculous potential of the Internet, there is nearly a limitless supply of potential clients all over the world.

Erik's list now includes the Hong Kong Trade Association, Northeastern University, SurgeryU (the Internet's largest video library of minimally invasive gynecologic surgery), and many others. The company cost under $200 to start and now supports Erik's family. And remember what we said about revenue streams? Each of Erik's clients can be considered a separate revenue stream. If he loses one client, the business does not fail. His risk is low, making it easier for him to succeed.

At the same time that Erik was building EPR Creations, he also started pursuing his love of music to a greater degree. Erik began playing in restaurants and bars around the Atlanta area with different musicians. He had the chance to play violin with artists such as Collective Soul and Zac Brown. He also conducted studio recordings for India Arie, Anthony David, and Tamar Davis, several of which were nominated for Grammy Awards. This is an entirely new revenue stream.

Here's an important point about entrepreneurship. Spending less time commuting to work, hanging around the office to impress the boss, and gossiping at the water cooler frees you to pursue your other interests. These could be hobbies, sports, travel, or starting second and third businesses. If you, like Erik, can find one business to pay the bills, you may have the time and money to start a second or third business. And there is no telling where that might lead you. You might very well find hidden talents you never knew you had. And remember that having your own business allows you to multitask easily. While waiting for one customer to return an e-mail, you can be working on a separate project for your other businesses, simply toggling from one computer screen to another. Try that in a corporate office, and see where it would get you. Also, as an entrepreneur, you have the luxury of setting your own hours, working early in the morning, late at night, or on weekends, providing the flexibility it takes to launch several businesses.

Erik has added yet another revenue stream into his business: SEO expert. SEO stands for "search engine optimization" and is the art of getting your website to rank number one on a Google search. Any website that ranks super high on Google should be making lots of money for its owners. Getting to number one on Google is a millionaire maker. Success in the natural, organic rankings is the way to build traffic for your site. Google ads are expensive, and in the long term, we prefer spending the money and time on a long-term SEO strategy. For Erik, this extra revenue stream helps him diversify risk and is yet another way to use the Net to make money.

LESSON #20

SEO is the art of appearing high on Google searches. Paying for Google ads drives up costs and is not the best way to build Web traffic. Changing keywords in the content, coding, and making other aspects of your website more efficient is usually more cost-effective.

Search Engine Optimization and Page Rank

While starting an SEO business might not be for you, this idea brings us to a topic that needs to be discussed. The authors of this book are proud to be among Erik's many clients, and that is because search engine optimization is very important. We hired Erik to work on our Google ranking and to teach our students how to achieve high Google rankings. Please make sure you use the free month of membership on our website, The Entrepreneur School (http://www.the entrepreneurschool.com), which is included with the purchase of this book, and take Erik's classes on getting your website to appear first when a Web browser uses a search engine.

Your website's page rank (PR) largely determines your Google ranking. Google assigns a score for each Web page, from 10 as the high to 1 as the low. Page rank tells you how important your website is, in the "mind" of Google. UPS (with its millions of daily users) has a PR of 8, for example. Most sites score a 2 or 3. In a small niche— say, selling spice racks online—a 3 is high enough to generate enough sales to make the business successful. For a more competitive niche, a 4 or 5 is necessary. For most of us, a 5 should be the goal, meaning a website that will generate enough revenue to live off. To learn your website's page rank, you must install the Google Toolbar on your browser. Search for "Google Toolbar," and the first link in the results will take you to the site that allows you to add the toolbar to Safari or Internet Explorer. All entrepreneurs must know their PR, just as they know their marketing budget, cost of sales, and names of their best customers' kids.

LESSON #21

Entrepreneurs must work to manipulate their Google-calculated page rank (PR), to ensure they are on the first page for their keywords.

Page rank can be increased by improving the content of your page and by increasing the number of other sites that link to you. Content is critical. The content on your website should use the right words to ensure that your site comes up on a Google search. These are called keywords. Keywords are the words that users type into Google to search for you or other companies that deliver the kinds of products or services they're interested in. If you are selling fancy dinner china, you may think your keyword is *china*. But if you type "china" into Google, all the results will be about the country of China, not about dinnerware. *Dinnerware* might be a better keyword for you. So the content on your page should use the word *dinnerware*, as opposed to *china*. Make sure to use your keywords early and often on the site.

LESSON #22

Your page rank is determined by (1) the content of your page and the correct use of keywords and (2) the number of sites that link to you. Both of these can be manipulated to increase your score and revenue.

Sites that link to your website are called backlinks. Increasing the number of backlinks to your site also is critical. Think about it: site A has ten sites that link to it (backlinks), and site B has one hundred backlinks. The market has voted and says site B is more important. The process of increasing your backlinks, called link building, is critical to almost every entrepreneur. Again, please use your free month at The Entrepreneur School website, and watch the videos on how to get one hundred sites to link to you.

All the entrepreneurs introduced in this book use the Net as a powerful tool. No matter what your business, you will need a strong Web component. Go ahead and start learning the basics of programming and search engine optimization. You quite possibly will base your new business on the Internet, so the skills of PR and keywords will be critical to you. A Web business starts quickly and cheaply, but it will succeed only if you play the Google game to build a site that lots of people can find.

7

The "Wow" Factor

THE VALUE PROPOSITION IS THE CORNERSTONE upon which you will build your business. Simply said for a business owner, it is that which you do better than anyone else in the world. What makes your business sexy, unique, and compelling? What in your company makes customers say, "Wow"? As a business owner, you can better compete by having a unique value proposition, one that is so distinctive, so compelling, so provocative that you stand out from everyone else. The value proposition must be clearly defined.

Put another way, your business idea must solve a problem that people didn't know they had, or it should solve an old problem in a new way. Use this chapter to test the idea you developed in Chapter 3 to see whether or not it fits this deceptively simple criterion. Every successful business solves a problem. The problem may be inadequate education on running technique, the lack of a local Alabama beer, the lack of a great knife store, or the lack of the perfect, cheap bar, but a problem is being solved. Ask yourself, "Does my business idea solve the problem I see?"

LESSON #23

The value proposition is what you do better that anyone else. To get the most business possible, you will have to articulate your value proposition very clearly.

The Customer Experience

A business idea is not enough. Obviously, something more is needed—something we see in successful businesses large and small. Take, for example, a simple grass cutting. Many high school students have cut grass. But is their ability to do so unique or compelling enough to motivate the students to grow a business out of it or to allow them to get customers? What value can high school students offer their neighbors?

One student had his dad drive him to a group of day laborers so he could hire four to six people to cut his neighbors' lawns. The student's value proposition was reliability, consistency, and stability. The neighbors could count on having the same familiar crew, on time, each week. Where the average student might be cutting one to three lawns per week, this young entrepreneur was cutting ten to fifteen lawns with the help of the laborers. Another approach to creating a unique appeal in this instance would be to diversify your services offered. Instead of asking for $20 a lawn, these business-minded kids could also offer to wash the neighbor's car or mow their lawn without asking for a set price. "I am raising money to go to Washington, D.C., to see Congress in session," they could say. "I will let you decide how much to help with my trip." Most times, the kid will get paid more than $20 this way.

This is how a value proposition is created. Cutting the grass is now about more than just the grass; it's about helping a kid's education. That's a value proposition anyone can support, regardless of how little you care about grass.

In testing the value proposition of a business, we often like to ask what is unique about it. What will this business provide that will differentiate it from all others? It is critically important for the business owner to be able to answer this question. A new business has to be able to stand the differentiation test. Tread lightly, though. It isn't enough to be able to say what you think makes you unique; you also have to show how the uniqueness is relevant to the customer.

For instance, in the lawn care example, the high school entrepreneur can't just say he employs six day laborers, which is a unique arrangement for a high schooler. He has to explain how those six employees add value to his customers. What he has done with them is create a consistent and professional business that services the customers each week. So the question has two parts: (1) How are you unique? and (2) How is the uniqueness relevant to the customer? Hiring six workers is relevant to customers because they get their lawn cut each week reliably and at a good price. You have to answer both of these questions in a powerful way.

The customer experience must permeate the value proposition. Remember that it does not matter what the business owner thinks; it matters only what the customer thinks. Peter Drucker once said that nothing happens in the business until a customer pays for something. A business is not real until it has money coming in. Thus, the focus has to be completely customer-centric, and the business must be defined all around the customer. This is the only way to create enduring equity in the business.

As a business owner, if you can't describe what sets you apart, you need to stop and figure it out. Don't worry about your advertising, your website, business cards, logo, or the language for your marketing materials. Take time to write down all that makes your business unique. Answer these questions:

- What is the coolest thing about your business?
- What is the sexiest thing about your business?
- What is the most unique and compelling thing you offer over and above your competitors?

If it's hard for you to identify the one thing that makes your business different, then it doesn't matter what your image looks like. Customers will see the lack of value and stop buying what you're selling—if they ever even started. Jack Welch, two-decade CEO of General Electric, said, "If you don't have a competitive advantage, don't compete." In evaluating business ideas, if you can't define what your competitive advantage is (that would be your value proposition), then move on to a different business opportunity.

Creating the Value Proposition

In this section you will find a process to develop a value proposition that is both compelling and provocative. To start, gather some friends, family, and customers, order some pizza, get some drinks—anything to create a fun environment. Once the conversation gets rolling, steer it toward your business idea. Try to get everybody to list all the factors that affect a customer's opinion of your business. We call these factors the "perception makers." We'll use an example of a bookstore. This exercise will help you define how to make your business different from the competition and more valuable to customers.

With your group, list every element that gives the customer a perception of your business. Using our bookstore example, we have the following list:

- Location
- Website
- Building
- Word of mouth
- Furniture
- Shelves
- What it smells like
- Types of books
- Logo
- Brand
- Family-friendliness
- Coffee shop presence
- Exterior
- Parking
- Accessibility
- Hours
- Signage
- Greetings upon entrance
- Products offered
- Amenities
- Payment terms
- Packaging
- Frequent-buyer programs
- Author events

Remember the rules of brainstorming. There aren't any bad ideas; just focus your group on the customer experience from every conceivable angle. This initial brainstorming session can take about an hour, which is why it is important to create a fun and lively environment.

The next step will take more time. Once you've exhausted every possible way a customer might perceive your business, turn your focus to asking what you can do to really *wow* your customer for each of these. The following three questions will help guide you:

1. What might exceed the customer's expectations?
2. What is possible to do but not necessarily being done?
3. What has nobody attempted to do for their customers?

You don't want your customers leaving merely satisfied. Having customers who are merely satisfied is a problem. Satisfaction is the bare minimum for customers. When you have spent your hard-earned money on something, be it a product or a service, do you not expect to be satisfied? In describing a restaurant, if someone says, "I was satisfied," are you going to be compelled to visit? Now, if they say, "It was amazing!" how much more likely are you to go? Your goal for the exercise is to shoot for what will make your customers say, "Wow." For each possible way that a customer can create an impression of your business, you'll want to list what the customer expects and then what you can do to exceed these expectations—to have customers say, "Wow."

Let's go back to the bookstore. What do customers expect from a bookstore parking lot? They expect a large blacktop space with white lines and standard parking spaces. They expect it to be clean, well marked, and full of cars. Now we are going to focus on the parking lot and how we can wow our customers with it. Here are some interesting ways to improve parking that we've heard when we've done this exercise:

- Special areas for expecting mothers
- Covered parking
- A car wash
- Subsidized parking
- Valet parking
- Bookmobile parked out front
- Outdoor shopping areas
- A drive-through

Not all of these ideas are realistic, but the point of this exercise is to think outside the box and consider every option.

Once you've been through each perception maker, pick three to four items that will create the strongest impression on the customer, and figure out how you would put them into action once you launch your business. Would you offer valet parking? Would you have outdoor shopping areas? Continue to do this until you've implemented all possible items. The power of this exercise isn't in coming up with any one answer but in the collection of answers and in the process of putting yourself in your customer's shoes.

Many of the ideas you come up with will be challenging to implement, but your commitment to making an extraordinary customer experience will separate you from your competitors. Our experience has shown us that most businesses ignore this radical commitment to the customer. You are striving to create the difference that will allow your customers to choose you over the multitude of businesses they could choose. This style of value-based differentiation is advantageous because it allows you to charge a slight premium. We discussed earlier that our focus is not on figuring out how to be the cheapest option, but on how to be the best. Being the best certainly allows you to charge more.

This exercise is designed to ingrain value proposition into every facet of your business as you build it from scratch. The goal is for you to think about your value proposition in every decision you make in starting the business, from the location of the store to parking, inventory, appearance, and even the aroma. Whenever possible, you should try to make decisions that ensure that customers always get a little extra by choosing to spend their money with you. The time to incorporate this mind-set is in the very early planning stages of the business.

Chris's Value Proposition

One of the authors of this book, Chris, owned a painting business a decade ago. When starting the business, he employed the very exercise we just described. He created a baseline of his customers' expectations. What did they expect from a painter? Primarily, they expected a detailed estimate where the job was done on time in a clean and professional manner. At a minimum, he built the business to accomplish those things. Next, he listed all the things he could do to exceed his customers' expectations. Chris wanted them to say, "Wow!" when he left the job, so they would tell their neighbors about him. He wanted that critical word-of-mouth advertising boost, so he instilled a culture around this.

Customers probably couldn't tell the difference between a good paint job and an excellent paint job, but they could definitely sense the difference in their experience of the service. For one thing, Chris noticed that customers were offended when the painter used their restroom. The thought of their bathroom being used by a dirty worker seemed to affect them emotionally more than the incremental quality difference of a good paint job verses a great paint job. He instituted a policy that the painters could not use customers' restrooms.

What's the first impression a painter usually makes on a customer? It is the painter's arrival at the front door. Knowing this, Chris trained his painters to approach the situation in the friendliest manner possible. They would ring the doorbell, step back, and turn to the side. This created a more inviting first impression. Usually the customers who answered the door were young mothers, and Chris strove to charm them out of any fears about the laborers. He wanted to create the least-threatening interaction possible, and he did.

Another important perception maker for this business was scheduling. Most at-home contractor services tended to put their schedule ahead of the customer's schedule. Chris did it the other way around. If his customer's child had a naptime in the afternoon, he scheduled around that time. This showed customers that he valued their time more than his own. It was all about creating a customer experience that would make more of a noticeable difference than simply painting the house to a satisfactory level.

Chris did a number of other things that created a culture for the painters to wow the customers. He paid painters by the job, meaning speed was not the driver, but rather quality. He set up a competition among the painters that rewarded them for going above and beyond the call of duty for the customer. Chris also built into the quote two extra hours of the painters' time to do something to make the customer say, "Wow!" The painters were supposed to use the two extra hours in some creative way to serve the customer. Each week, he had a team meeting and shared all the different painters' "wow" solutions. The painters did other tasks like fixing garbage disposals, washing windows, and painting yard furniture at no charge—all in an effort to go that extra mile. Whoever was the most outstanding would be chosen as the weekly winner, with the winner receiving sports tickets or a dinner at Ruth's Chris Steak House.

Not all painting customers were right for Chris's company. A bank that needed foreclosed homes painted or a home investor would not be interested in the service value of his company. Those clients' primary value considerations are price and timeliness. This is why defining your target market is critical. Just as there is a spectrum of customers, there is a spectrum of value provided to those customers.

Chris's company didn't just say it put customers first; it actually paid painters and set up its billing to fulfill that promise. Chris systematically built processes across the business to support his value proposition. Because he created such a strong differentiation within his target market, his biggest competitors weren't other painting companies, but other ways his potential clients could spend their discretionary money. It came down to the customer asking, "Do I paint the house, take a vacation at Walt Disney World, or buy a new living-room set?" If they decided on painting their house, he was always the first choice. The difference created by his value proposition was managed through every step of the customer process.

Testing Your Idea

This section provides a list of rules you should follow to test your value proposition to see if it is truly sexy, provocative, and compelling. You can do this by simply holding an informal focus group with friends, neighbors, and relatives and presenting your value proposition to them. Or you can present the ideas to coworkers around the water cooler or the parents of your children's friends on the sidelines of soccer games. Better yet, test the idea in the real marketplace. Remember, we strongly recommend starting with one sale, one job, and slowly building your business. Use those first few jobs for research, to test whether your value proposition is truly resonating.

Value Proposition Rule #1: Don't Try to Satisfy Everybody

If you get no reaction—pro or con—from your value proposition, then it's probably an imitation. It's already out there in the marketplace. Forget wowing anyone. You must continue refining your value proposition to the point where it's so distinctive that it resonates powerfully with a certain few—the group you are trying to reach. This is your target market. As your business slowly grows, you will find yourself learning what works and what doesn't. You will learn what the customers value and what they don't. You can then slowly refine your business based on this early feedback.

If your business doesn't resonate powerfully or distinctly with your target market, then you'll end up mirroring your competition and looking like another imitation to the customer. If this is the case, your business will end up being a commodity business—and the only thing that distinguishes one commodity business from another is price.

Value Proposition Rule #2: Be Hired for Being the Best, Not the Cheapest

You may think price always wins out when it comes to a customer's decision. However, emotion plays a very large role in a consumer's decisions, so competing on price is a losing battle. Do you want to compete with Walmart and its buying power? No, you do not. Being the best is a stronger position than offering the lowest price. Money is certainly important, because you want to stay competitive in your industry or niche, but it won't create a lasting value the way offering a superior service does. What will get you hired is being the best at a competitive price.

Remember earlier, the story of the company Chris launched selling trucks to Vietnam? After learning that Vietnamese families often slept in the back of the trucks, he installed new bedding in each one to distinguish his product from the competition. He was able to price a little bit more aggressively at that point. It is always good to add value to a product whenever possible to give your company a competitive edge. Jim did as much with his computer camp by adding the prestige of Stanford University and MIT. Price is certainly important, because you want to stay competitive. But it won't create lasting value, as you will by offering superior service. Ten years later, customers remember going to MIT. They don't remember getting a cheap price. Also, striving to be the best is a great deal more rewarding than constantly finding ways to cut costs and lower prices.

Value Proposition Rule #3: Sell What Sells— Not Necessarily the Product

A while back, Chris was involved in helping a flooring franchise redesign its value proposition. In first working with them, he observed the company's primary business process. The franchise owner usually acted as the salesperson and would use a flooring van. He would bring samples of flooring out of the van and go into the home to show potential customers the different flooring options. The owner tended to talk to customers in terms the customer didn't really care about. The pitch included things like interlocking hardwood, the location of the manufacturers, different flooring specs, and many other technical aspects. Did any of this really resonate with the customer, though?

What was primarily wrong with the sales pitch? The flooring company's owner didn't understand what the company was really selling or to whom it was selling. The primary customer for the flooring was typically a homemaker who might be less inclined to know the technicalities. The first disconnect, then, was the fact that the salespeople were trying to sell the flooring on technical flooring specs. Basically, they were selling floors based on what they wanted, not on what their customer wanted.

The first task was to get the flooring company owner to understand what the customers really wanted and thus what the company was really selling. What the customers really wanted was to make their home beautiful. They wanted to hear about space, color, texture, and design. The owner of the flooring company needed to focus on selling beauty, not necessarily floors. Beauty was the value proposition.

You must understand who your customers are and what they want. In the example of the flooring company, flooring and flooring installation are the company's product, but what the company is really selling is beauty. So the value proposition must tell the customers why and how the company will make their home beautiful. Often, as you build the business, it becomes harder to maintain the necessary customer-centric focus. You get more isolated from the customer, because you are viewing situations from within the company. It is a strong temptation to take the view of the business owner, to think you are operating your business efficiently and doing all you can to serve your customers. But the customer perception can be dramatically different. That's why you must always focus on that customer perception.

Value Proposition Rule #4: Establish Credibility

Is your value proposition convincing and believable? When a customer reads it, sees it, or experiences it, does it pass the smell test? Ford claims the 2011 Taurus sedan is "America's most innovative full-size sedan." Do you believe this? For years, the Ford Taurus was touted as a reliable and stable car. OK, sure, we'll give them that. We buy in. But how about the most *innovative* car in America? Is it even more innovative than the new electric cars? Not a chance. There's an immediate credibility problem with Ford's value proposition.

It all comes down to the right packaging. If Lady Gaga's record label tried to brand her as America's Sweetheart, would the company be taken seriously? Yeah, right! This is the same reason we find it difficult to believe the politician who claims that a new law will reduce Washington's power. A business must be credible to the customer. There's always going to be initial skepticism among customers that the entrepreneur must overcome. It starts with the value proposition. If this is not credible, or if the message about your value is not credible, then your business will not be viewed as credible.

Remember that you can't just claim you're compelling and provocative; you must be able to prove it through interactions with customers. The use of certain details can help in building credibility. You have to be careful not to use too many details or the wrong kind of details, or you may dilute your message. For instance, it would not have been a good idea for salespeople in Chris's flooring business to focus on the granular density of the wood, compared with a competitor's wood. That would be overly technical, confusing, and distracting.

Statistics can be a good source of credibility, though, if you use them only to illustrate relationships. Let's say you want to illustrate the danger of deer to humans. You could use a number of statistics demonstrating deaths caused by deer. Or you could ask, "Which is more likely to kill a person, a shark or a deer?" The answer, of course, is a deer. Interestingly, a deer is three hundred times more likely to kill you than a shark. So the relationship between the deer-caused deaths versus the shark-caused deaths builds a more credible connection. The goal in using statistics is to build credibility only; don't overuse them, as they are pretty boring.

Value Proposition Rule #5: Be Different and Relevant

As a business, you want to be both relevant to your customers' life and differentiated to the point that there is no substitute for you. You want to create and identify the difference between you and your competitors. This difference should be well pronounced, shown, felt, measured, and managed every step of the way.

The goal should be to make your customer remember your value proposition—that one thing that separates your business from other businesses. Recall Joey Tatum, the bar owner in Athens? He created a bar scene that has its own unique atmosphere. His bar's culture went against the grain of the typical bar. In that regard, he catered to a slightly older demographic. His bar was designed for adults living in the community, rather than college students, solving the locals' problem of where to go if they want to enjoy a drink without being surrounded by nineteen-year-olds trying to trick the bartender into serving them. The value proposition is very simple: no college kids.

The temptation for business owners is to answer all the questions customers may ask. They want to be full-service, to add value in all these different ways. You can hear and see this in entrepreneurs who are all over the map with their business ideas. At the end of the day, they've lost the investors, as they can't identify the value proposition. They say the thing that distinguishes jazz musicians is the notes they don't play. They strip the music down and prioritize the music around a certain melody. Like a jazz musician, the entrepreneur must be a master of exclusion. Focus on what differentiates the business—the one thing you want your customer to remember.

Value Proposition Rule #6: Compose the Mental Image of Your Business

As you are starting your business, and even when it is up and running, you must always take the pulse of your customer. An important tool you can use to maintain customer focus is the mental-image process. Basically, you're trying to ascertain the mental image that your customers have of your business once they've finished doing business with you. Then compare this mental image with your value proposition. The best-case scenario in this comparison is that the two come out the same. The customer's mental image of your company would be in effect repeating the company's value proposition.

Constantly stay in touch with people external to your business who can answer exactly how and what you are conveying to the customer. Ask them what they think of your business. Go back to your value proposition, and see if it is still reaching the customer the way it once did. Perhaps you may not even know that you've lost the pulse of your target market. This is the most dangerous place to be as an entrepreneur. It's like the emperor without his clothes. Here, the entrepreneur is strolling merrily on his way with his business, while not reaching the customers at all. To avoid this, start and maintain an attitude that defines all things around the customer. Adopt an attitude in which you are willing to be wrong and are committed to learning constantly.

Value Proposition Rule #7: Identify with the Customer's Feelings and Passions

When people purchase something, they make a decision based on feelings. It doesn't matter if the customer is a teenage girl buying an outfit or a business executive buying a luxury car. Emotions play a very strong role in the transaction. With the clothes, the girl is thinking how she feels with the clothes on, what people will think of her, etc. Similar emotions come into play with almost any other product.

So, in understanding the power of emotions, even in seemingly logical or numbers-based decisions, the entrepreneur must hook people emotionally. Of course, this starts in the value proposition. Does the value of your business, product, or service hook your customers' emotions? The kid's lawn business we mentioned at the beginning of the chapter does. Remember, getting your lawn mowed satisfies your need for a nice lawn, but what makes you feel great is that you are helping send the kid to Washington, D.C., furthering his education.

We are no strangers to the use of emotions in garnering support for something. Think about the way Coke advertises at Christmastime. It is a heavy play on the emotions surrounding Christmas. Do you recall all the different messages following the tragic earthquake in Haiti? Presidents, a First Lady, musicians (Jay-Z, Justin Timberlake, Bono), businesses, and nonprofits told us to send help to those in Haiti. Their plea was based on our emotions, which would need to be tugged in order to get us to help those who were suffering. It was a powerful message, and we responded accordingly.

Now, we're not suggesting that you necessarily need a cause attached to your value proposition, but the goal is to build an emotional connection between your business and its customers. Without that connection to your business or product, your customers will view your offering as just another business. Focus on a few tactics to help build an emotional connection. While forming your value proposition, you, as the entrepreneur, must be emotionally focused on what you're doing for your customers. Answer this question: Why is the world a better place because my business exists?

Value Proposition Rule #8: Wow Your Customers

As an entrepreneur, if you do the unexpected for your customers, they will remember your business. Once, when Chris was traveling for a consulting engagement, he stayed in a hotel outside Philadelphia. It was late, and there weren't any restaurants open. The vending machine at the hotel was broken, and he asked the lady at the front desk if there was any other place he could get something to eat. Unfortunately, she knew of nothing else. Chris went up to his room and, after fifteen minutes, heard a knock at the door. The person who had checked him in was standing there with a bottle of water and some cookies. Is it a surprise that he still remembers that hotel to this day?

This is a compelling story of customer service; it was not expected at all to see the lady standing there with a bottle of water and cookies. As he traveled for that engagement, he continued to stay at the same hotel chain because of the value of the company's customer service. He might not recall the advertising, the logo, or the signage, but he will never forget the level of customer service.

Being unexpected is the most basic way to get somebody's attention. Doing something unexpected breaks the person's pattern of thought and is more likely to trigger a wow moment. Think how we all love a movie with a surprise ending. In identifying your value proposition, think of ways to offer your customers extras that are unexpected. That adds even more value. An unexpected gift always has more impact than a routine, predictable one.

8

Marketing
Your Product

MANY FORMS OF TRADITIONAL ADVERTISING are not as effective as they were twenty years ago, particularly for small businesses. The Internet has captured the attention of so many consumers, and it allows better targeting of an audience than the shotgun approach of billboards and newspaper advertising. The online world of Google, Facebook, and social media is now the norm for small business marketing.

Marketing on the Internet

In a perfect world, either you had a business idea before you picked up this book, or you finished Chapter 3 (on finding business ideas) with one in mind. For you to get that idea off the ground, however, your first goal should be to sell something. Remember, a business is not a business until you've sold something. Marketing your business requires a different approach, though, depending on whether you are selling a service or selling a product. For a service business, marketing means getting your first customer, exceeding that customer's expectations, and then finding more customers. Your first customer may be a friend or relative, but you can surprise him or her by doing an over-the-top terrific job. As that customer hands you a check, politely ask him or her to tell anyone else who needs work done that you are available, and offer your card. The word-of-mouth referral that can result from this transaction is marketing at its most primitive level, but it is still powerful marketing. You have marketed your product by doing a good job, building a solid reputation, and handing a business card to a happy customer.

For a product-based business, you will do much of your marketing on the Internet, which is also where you will sell your products. The trick is learning enough about Google and Facebook marketing, search engine optimization, and social media implantation to ensure a constant stream of visitors to your website. We teach all of these skills throughout this book, but more analysis is available at our website, The Entrepreneur School (http://www.theentrepreneurschool.com), as well.

LESSON #24

We have found that advertising on Facebook is 75 percent cheaper than it is on Google, and it's also quite effective.

Right now, one of the hottest avenues to market your product online is Facebook advertising. The major advantage of Facebook ads is the cost, which can stretch your marketing budget a long way. Facebook ads can cost 75 percent less than a Google ad, and they are effective. In addition to the lower price, advertising on Facebook allows you to reach a much more targeted audience. Say you are selling wedding productions. You can advertise to Facebook users who have recently changed their status to "engaged." The downside of Facebook ads is that you are pitching your products to an audience that is not directly searching for anything, as a Google user is. Facebook surfers are like TV viewers—engaged in an outside activity and perhaps resentful of being intruded upon by an ad. In any case, Facebook is low-cost and effective, which is why it's flourishing as one of the newest trends in advertising.

Getting the Message Right

Part of marketing is boiling your message down to its most concise form. Through trial and error, you will have to learn the best elevator pitch for closing a sale in thirty seconds, and the perfect price. The perfect price is the lowest you can afford while also turning a profit. We'll talk more about pricing later. As we've said, what's more important than price is what you have to offer and how you represent it in your materials.

As a new entrepreneur, no matter what you are selling and how you are selling it, you'll discover that it's easy to get caught up in the details of starting a business—legal, accounting, website design and copy. These things are important, but they all have to be put in the context of sales. Remember, it's all about sales.

In our low-risk approach to starting up a business, marketing may start one-on-one between the owner and potential customers. Perhaps the owner sells only at trade shows, pitching the product directly to one customer at a time. How do you grow from this personalized sales approach to an effective ad campaign reaching thousands every day?

When Jim and Doug were building their computer camp business, they quickly learned they were really selling happiness to kids who might not have fit in all that well in their respective schools. The target market basically consisted of children who were happier in front of a computer and had few friends. (To be more precise, the target market was those kinds of children, but especially those who also went to private school and had two parents working highly skilled jobs.) Early on, Jim and Doug thought they were selling education, when in fact they were really selling acceptance for socially challenged kids and peace of mind for their parents. Reflecting that proposition in the marketing was difficult. You can't simply write ad copy that promises, "Fun for dorky kids."

The company's sales materials and process changed. The initial marketing effort centered on the wow factor of cool technology, a camp that would make your kid smart. But in conversations with parents, Jim and Doug discovered that the camp's hidden niche was helping parents find a place where their shy kids would fit in. Jim and Doug trained their phone operators to say that they understood that type of kid, that they had been shy themselves when they were growing up, and that they knew how important it is to draw kids out of their shells. This empathetic approach had a big impact. When parents called to ask any question, they usually ended up finishing the conversation having purchased a week at camp. Focusing on the benefits of the product or service is much more compelling than focusing on its features.

Here's another example, of marketing materials for a fitness center: "Our fitness center, which is just for adults, has sixteen exercise classes, a pool that is available for water aerobics and open swims, and full spa and massage service." The message tells the customers the features of the product and focuses on a target market. The problem is that it doesn't describe how those features are relevant or beneficial to the customer. It forces customers to figure out on their own how the features will change or add value to their life. You don't want customers to have to do work in their heads to understand the product's value.

Consider this slightly reworded example: "Our fitness center features classes and exercise equipment that help adults maintain their fitness and lead healthier, happier lives." This message mentions some features but then puts greater emphasis on what those features do for the target market: provide a healthy life.

LESSON #25

When you are marketing your business, it's important to focus on the benefits of the product or service over the methods used to achieve them.

In writing marketing materials, avoid clichés. Here are some that should never be included because they are simply overused and therefore have little impact on potential customers:

- "Premier"—Describing your business as the premier source for anything is far too common.
- "State of the art"—This attribute is vague and empty sounding.
- "Combined 100 years of experience"—If anything, this just communicates that the business is owned by older people.
- "Second to none"—This is just another way to say "premier," and it's a meaningless boast.

Instead of empty language, why not actually provide hard evidence of your accomplishments in the description of your business? For example, if you have a weight loss clinic, tell customers that 90 percent of clients lose thirty pounds within six months. Or you can say, "Our customers pay on average 30 percent less for the product than the national average price."

Once you have removed all the clichés and have a clear and compelling message to your target audience, there are many ways to deliver it: advertising, public relations, personal selling, men in chicken suits holding signs on street corners. We will get to those methods in a moment.

Making a Permanent Marketing Plan Through Trial and Error

When enough profits come in, you can slowly test other marketing efforts to ensure that your instincts were right. Marketing is easy to test. Either you get sales from the marketing, or you don't. You know immediately if your phone is ringing after an ad runs. There are many ways to find out where your customers are coming from, including simply asking, "How did you hear about us?" You will need a permanent marketing plan that guarantees income, thereby reducing risk. One pet peeve we have with marketing plans occurs when they seem guided by the idea that "if we capture just 1 percent of the market, we will make $15 million in sales in year one." Statements like this are the epitome of amateur. The thought behind it is on the right track, but just how will you capture 1 percent of the market? It is not at all easy to do.

Low-risk entrepreneurs ask instead, "How much money do I want to take home?" In this regard, the marketing plan is intrinsically related to the business plan in general. For example, take a flooring business with a net profit margin of 20 percent. For the owner to take home $100,000 in annual profit, the business has to generate $500,000 in sales. Considering that an average job would be worth at the very least $2,500, the business owner needs two hundred jobs a year to ensure $100,000 per year in profit. Now, if at least 30 percent of customers who meet with a salesperson end up buying the product, you need to schedule 667 appointments with customers. Breaking that down by week, 13 appointments per week will generate a $100,000 annual profit.

The challenge is finding the leads and closing the sales. The owners of the flooring business analyze all marketing tactics to see how to generate and sustain seventy monthly leads. What are marketing tactics? They are actions we can take to market our product or service, as we mentioned earlier:

- Direct-mail brochures targeted to specific zip codes in neighborhoods where you have found success in landing customers
- Cold-calling campaigns where you or your sales staff knock on doors in select neighborhoods and pitch the product
- TV and radio advertising
- Internet ads
- Public relations efforts, generating news stories about your product by pitching the idea to newspapers, radio stations, magazines, and television stations
- A blog about your product
- Word of mouth, which can be accomplished simply by telling happy customers to tell their neighbors about your product or by talking it up at soccer games and other events
- Yard signs—for work performed at a home, a sign placed in the front yard so that neighbors who need similar work will spot it almost always generates more jobs

All these tactics create credible leads. Each marketing effort will reach a certain number of people, cost a certain amount for each person reached, and then generate a certain number of leads.

Let's take two examples—one whose revenue generation can be "proven" in a fairly straightforward way, and one for which it is more difficult to do so. Let's start with direct mail, as the results tend to be measurable. In this case, let's say the response rate is 0.2 percent, and we are going to send out ten thousand direct-mail fliers. This will yield twenty responses or leads. Given our close rate of 30 percent, twenty responses will net six jobs. But you must count on 20 percent of the sales being dropped as customers shop around for a better price or change their minds (a behavior called abandonment). That leaves us with five jobs for the month, producing $12,000 in monthly revenue. Let's use a cost of fifty cents per flier. That would mean the direct-mail campaign would cost $5,000 and bring in $12,000 of revenue.

That may not sound good, but direct mail or any direct-marketing program also creates a secondary marketing impact. If you look only at the cost and the direct impact on revenue, then you're not looking at the whole picture. Every customer creates an opportunity to put a sign in the customer's front yard, both literally and figuratively. You've gained that customer for life and get all of the customer's referrals. So the secondary impact of the direct mail is that it will generate other customers through word of mouth.

With just one tactic, we've landed five jobs. We need another twelve to hit our monthly target, requiring us to look at another tactic that isn't as measurable. In addition to direct mail, we could employ an Internet site that provides leads to service providers and charges them on a per-lead basis. There are numerous companies that provide such a service, such as ServiceMagic (http://www.servicemagic .com). Let's assume the cost is $35 a lead. How do we know how many people are going to go to this portal per month and request our services? There are ways we can estimate the number of leads, but how can you have the certainty? Admittedly, you can't. However, is it reasonable to assume that at least one job per month will result from this tactic? Probably.

With just two marketing tactics, we have created six jobs a month. Remember, we need seventeen jobs to ensure our goal is reached. Using this method, we would step through as many marketing tactics as we need to reach our goal of seventeen jobs. For each tactic, we would repeat the same type of analysis as we did on the direct-mail and Internet tactics. The idea is to figure out the number of people reached by the marketing tactic and then percentage of people that become leads.

Once we've outlined the marketing tactics that generate sufficient leads in securing our seventeen jobs, we've completed our marketing plan. We've created a road map to follow. We know exactly what we need to do each month to generate our sales. This will allow us to prioritize our schedules down to the day. Once the plan is in place, you'll know that on any given day, you'll be starting a marketing campaign, calling a customer, tracking appointments, etc.

The great thing about creating a plan like this is that success and control fall squarely on the entrepreneur's shoulders. Although it is frightening at first, the plan really allows the entrepreneur the control and freedom to drive the business. Most importantly, it reduces the risk. If the economy worsens, the plan doesn't change; the entrepreneur just has to work harder.

In a bad economy, response rates drop as customers will be more reluctant to spend. This means more direct mail, door hangers, trade shows, whatever it takes. This may be hard work, but it is under your control, and you will learn quickly what is effective and what is not generating revenue for your business. Then, when the economy recovers, as it surely will, your system is in place, your company's reputation and customer base are solid, and you are poised, not for $100,000 a year in profit, but for much more.

9

Reduce Risk by Reducing Inventory

YOU HAVE A BUSINESS, AND you're selling something. You have some sort of warehouse where you store your products: fifty of this, thirty-five of that, and twenty-eight of that. You have a big pile of stuff you're going to sell over time (you hope). However, what if instead of that arrangement, you never touched the product, never even purchased it until after you were paid by the customer? What if you never had to rent a warehouse or haul a shipment to the post office? What would happen is that you would reduce your risk by not having any inventory.

Drop Shipping

The practice of selling inventory you don't have is called drop shipping, and it can be a very solid low-risk business venture. What you do is purchase products from a third-party wholesaler only after you have sold them. The wholesaler handles all the shipping and also the returns. All you have to do is collect the money and maintain the website.

Selecting a Product

Jim created an exercise in which his students selected an industry and product, researched all the drop shippers, selected the best one, and designed a product mix for an imaginary website. One student started a site that sells anything with a college or pro sports team logo. The site sells seat cushions for specific stadiums, hats, jerseys, and other items. For each team, the student's company has about eighty to one hundred different products ready to sell, covering every professional sports team and many college teams as well. That's one hundred products for three hundred teams, an astronomical number of products to carry in inventory.

LESSON #26

Drop shipping is a great first business. A third party handles much of the risk and the entire inventory, while all you have to do is maintain the website and collect the money.

During class, this student selected products and found suppliers who were willing to ship directly to the customers. A simple way to find companies willing to do this is to use a search engine such as Google to look up the product name and peruse the websites of the companies that sell each product. Often, the website will include information on wholesale accounts and whether the company supplier is willing to drop ship. You can then either call or e-mail the company for more information on how to set up an account. For Jim's student, a big advantage of this method was that these wholesalers already had a license from the sports associations such as the

National Football League (NFL) and National Collegiate Athletic Association (NCAA) to sell the items. Those licenses would have taken years for a fledgling entrepreneur to get. In the end, the student selected seven drop shippers that were able to supply his entire product mix.

Many times, you will need to use multiple suppliers in order to get a broad range of products and to have backups when one supplier is out of stock. Having multiple suppliers also lowers your risk in case one of them becomes unreliable or goes out of business. Since the basic framework of your business is already in place, adding additional suppliers does not cause undue complication and enhances your product offerings.

LESSON #27

Get access to famous logos like Coca-Cola, the NFL, and hot movies by reselling from the right wholesaler. Some wholesalers already have license deals in place to sell branded wares.

In addition to merchandise, this student's company provided a wealth of useful and interesting sports information, including scores, injuries, etc., on its website. The site is updated several times a day, making it *sticky* (a term we defined in Chapter 6) and garnering more opportunities for sales and positive word of mouth in the process. Websites that have new content all the time get plenty of repeat visitors.

Informative blogs also help generate traffic for retail sites. People will come for the voice they've become a fan of, and once they get there, they find plenty of information, so they keep coming back.

Even a retail site should be designed with some kind of bonus draw, so customers want to check in for more reasons than just to buy something. A functional drop shipping site with a large free informational section is a great low-risk business. The only cost is building a website, which should be no more than $2,500. Aside from that, all you have to do is figure out what you want to sell.

LESSON #28

All websites should be sticky, meaning that they include interesting and relevant information that will encourage customers to spend more time on the site.

If you are going to start a business with drop shipping, though, it's important to find a product you will be able to make come up near the top of the Google search results. Some products would be very difficult to rank well on search engines, because the business is extremely competitive. There are lots of sellers who are Net savvy and are also making sure their products rank highly on Google. For other products, it will be much easier to get a high Google ranking because fewer companies are competing or the sellers simply have not caught on yet to the importance of a high Google ranking. At the website for The Entrepreneur School, Module 6 teaches about this techie stuff in greater detail. Check the website (http://www.theentrepreneurschool .com), and make sure you understand what this entails.

Selecting a Drop Shipper

There are good drop shippers and bad drop shippers, and you need to make sure you get the best one possible. To do that, you will want to research a list of twenty or more options before picking one. Go online, search for the type of product by name ("candle drop shipper," for example), and make a list of all the competitors. You will be shocked that there are as many as a hundred drop shippers in some niches. Compare the costs of using different drop shippers. Avoid any that are based overseas, since shipping takes much longer, and the company may be harder to get in touch with. Make sure the one you go with ships the same day you place an order and that it provides a telephone number so you can reach the company if something goes wrong.

There are a couple of other key points to consider when selecting a drop shipper. What is the shipper's inventory management system like? Does it have a system you can access every night to get a breakdown of inventory and therefore pull out-of-stock products off your website? Also, find out—even if takes a telephone call to the company—what kind of box the drop shipper sends the product in. A great drop shipper will use a box with your company's logo plastered on the side, a good drop shipper uses a plain box with nothing printed on it, and a bad drop shipper ships in its own box, which can confuse your customers, who thought they were buying directly from you.

Disadvantages of Drop Shipping

Drop shipping has many advantages, as we've already mentioned. The startup costs are low, there's no inventory or daily packing, and the risk is very low. Also, depending on the wholesaler's policies and sometimes your own credit rating and references from other suppliers, you may have thirty days or more before you have to pay—in essence, giving you a business loan. That's not to say drop shipping is without disadvantages. There are a few of these, too, that you should know about.

For one thing, with drop shipping, you are accepting a partial loss of control, because you are not physically in control of the product, and you can't personally ship it to the customer. Also, even though it may be cheaper than storing inventory yourself, the process itself can be expensive, and you likely will not get bulk discounts, because you are literally buying the merchandise piece by piece as it is shipped to individual customers. Additionally, you might have a problem with meeting certain demands when there's a middleman to contend with.

Let's say, for instance, in the case of Jim's student who started a sports merchandising website, the wholesaler suddenly ran out of hot items right when the website received a ton of orders. A problem like this would come into effect if the New York Yankees won the World Series and all of a sudden the wholesaler was out of Yankees merchandise for the next six weeks. There could be almost nothing worse for your business than a lack of supply at a key moment like that. The website would have already collected the money, and the customers would be anticipating getting their goods in three to five days, but—whoops—"We don't have any of those." This is how you get angry customers who are waiting for refunds and are likely never to place another order.

The wholesaler is going to incorporate into the price the time it takes to ship the products individually rather than sending a giant pallet of goods, which is easier and more efficient. The wholesaler is then going to take a huge chunk of the profits, too. The sports company would have to pay its drop shipper on average 6 percent, which could very easily make up half of the profit margin.

Drop shipping is not challenge-free, but it does fit into our model of low-risk entrepreneurship. Most importantly, by eliminating lots of the busywork, it gives you time to worry about growing your business. You can easily get a company up and running this way for $5,000 or less. Moreover, you can do so in less than three months and by working on it only at night after leaving your other, mortgage-paying job. You may not have the time to ship hundreds of packages each week or the money to buy a lot of inventory, but the drop shipper will. For an entrepreneur just starting out, this method can be a good entry point.

As you get bigger, you will be able to afford to hold inventory. Until then, drop shipping is a low-risk step toward building your own inventory. It allows you to test without risk. You can add a new product line to see if it sells well without buying inventory. Once you find out which products sell well, you can build your own inventory, buying in bulk, buying directly from China, and tactics like these. You also might need to get some help at that point, in the form of employees, which is what we'll be discussing in the next chapter.

10

Hiring
Employees

LET'S ASSUME YOU'VE GOTTEN YOUR business up and running. As sales grow, you will quickly reach the point at which you need help simply to get through the day. That is a great thing! While it may be stressful to be so busy, the fact that you need help means you've achieved some success.

Building a Team

Randy Brown, the law firm outsourcer, needed employees from day one to fulfill the services required by his clients. He knew in starting such a business that he would not be able to handle doing all that work himself. The "employees" he ended up using were temps, since he could not afford the costs of bringing on permanent employees. While the upside of service businesses is that it is possible to bootstrap them so easily and cheaply, the downside is that they require employees to grow. You can quickly and easily start a catering company—it's a perfect low-risk business—but in order to get past twenty cakes a week, you will need to build a team.

With the uncertainty about health care costs and potential new taxes on employers, most businesses are afraid to hire anyone. This position makes financial sense; after all, one of the best ways to destroy your low-risk startup is to bring on employees and their associated costs. We advise waiting as long as possible to incur these costs. However, when it is time to get a staff under you, it's important that you have a game plan.

This is how it should work: An entrepreneur gets an idea off the ground by working very diligently, designing the marketing plan, and generating sales. The business starts to grow, and the entrepreneur starts planning to accommodate growth. At this point, the entrepreneur is probably working the majority of the day and servicing all parts of the business, leaving little room for him or her to take on additional tasks to support growth. The entrepreneur starts building the business and planning for growth while remaining at the center of everything.

Growth will be capped purely by the hours that the entrepreneur can work in any given day. You could attempt to put systems and processes in place to increase productivity, but there are still only so many hours in a day and even fewer hours that one can actually work during it. The ability for the business and the entrepreneur to make money is limited by the entrepreneur being the primary "doer" of the business. To take the company into the phase where wealth is created, the entrepreneur has to move from being the doer of the business to being the owner. The owner must bring in the right people, and if the company grows large enough, the owner might also need to bring in management to execute the plan.

A business is really all about the people it hires, and these people can either make or break your business. Good ideas never succeed or fail by themselves; rather, they are helped along by the actions and inactions of others. A good idea can easily fail when born of the wrong people. When venture capitalists, angels, or other small business investors choose to make an investment, the people driving or managing the business are always the first and primary consideration. Conversely, the right team can monetize almost any idea.

The entrepreneur will have to learn how to build a team, including a management team and a group of lesser-skilled workers for shipping and manual labor. Not only will the business require more time than the entrepreneur can afford, but it will grow beyond the entrepreneur's abilities and skills. Entrepreneurs are by nature problem solvers and would rather do it themselves than pay others to do it; however, eventually any entrepreneur will realize that he or she can no longer handle the company alone and that full-time, real employees are needed. You will know it's time when you start feeling completely overwhelmed by the business or when you really start to sense that you are leaving profit on the table by not having a staff that would allow you to expand. Building a team will prepare the business for scaling up and will also allow the entrepreneur to move into an ownership role.

LESSON #29

When hiring employees, don't be afraid to take on someone who is better than you at a given task or more knowledgeable than you about a given subject. In fact, you should aim for such people.

The people an entrepreneur selects for his or her team will be used to measure both the business and the entrepreneur. The assembly of the team, then, is an indication of the extent to which the entrepreneur is open to advice and able to generate enthusiasm for the company. It's important to have a real strategy for conducting a search and then to go after only people who are better than you. Potential employees must share your vision for the future and agree how they will fit into the growth of the company. But most importantly, the early hires must drive revenue, either by growing operations or by bringing in new customers.

The entrepreneur is responsible for providing inspiration, instilling a vision of success, and incentivizing employees correctly. When setting up the incentive structure for the team, the business owner needs to consider all new employees while providing those future employees with an opportunity to share in the equity of the company. The owner must create and share a vision and then establish systems and processes that transfer to others the qualities that make him or her successful at being the doer. Thus, the business grows less dependent on the entrepreneur.

A helpful strategy is to set aside an options pool—shares of company stock that can be given to employees at a later date. This ties employees to the business and its success. Also, the business owner works to create motivation and incentives so that others care about the business as much as (if not more than) the entrepreneur. As the owner accomplishes this, the owner becomes free to focus on the target customer and optimize the design of the business around the customer.

Does Your Company Need Employees?

Before you get started looking for employees, give some more thought to whether or not you need them. For instance, the owners of an Internet sales company may never need employees. A couple who run a niche business selling vintage paperbacks and producing profit of a half million dollars a year might get along fine on their own. The owners may not want to grow the business, as the excess profits would not compensate for the decreased revenue share. Is an extra $50,000 in income worth the hassle of hiring and reporting employees? For this couple, it probably would not be worth it.

Costs associated with having employees are growing rapidly. For instance, under the new health care reform bill, companies with more than fifty employees will have to start offering health insurance in 2014 or pay a fine. Considering these costs, it may be best to let a successful business stagnate and have a great lifestyle business. A lifestyle business is one in which you don't have the hassles of making payroll every week; you can come and go whenever you please and simply shut down the business whenever you like with the click of a mouse. A drop shipping business, as described in the previous chapter, would be an example of this. You simply pay a contractor (the drop shipper) to do most of the work. Of course, as mentioned in Chapter 9, many costs and risks are associated with this strategy.

Or it may be best to use only temps forever. Temps can be hired for almost any job, but again there is a downside: you will likely have to pay a temp agency a commission, driving up the costs. Also, temps may never become as proficient at the job as some other prequalified candidates.

LESSON #30

Consider just using temporary workers rather than bringing on full-time employees. This decision could have a huge impact on your bottom line.

When determining whether you need employees, it's important to size up your business. Correlate a small business's size with hits to get on base in baseball. A single is a business that produces $50,000 in profit while the owner's health insurance (and extra income) is supplied by a primary job. A double is a lifestyle business with no employees, delivering health insurance for the owners and $100,000 in take-home income. A triple is $250,000 in income, a permanent employee or two, and several temp employees. A home run is ten employees with benefits and $500,000 in take-home pay for the owner. A grand slam? That would probably entail selling the business for over $10 million.

The takeaway here is that when you consider bringing on staff, you must acknowledge the base you are on and the base you are striving for. Not every double should be pushed into a triple. Jim and Doug's education business should have been left at around second-base size. It was producing great revenue with the accompanying lifestyle. As the business grew to hundreds of employees, though, the company's income went down because revenues had to be spread out a lot further.

Positions to Fill

If the business is generating under $5 million in revenue, do not hire a chief financial officer. You can handle the financial planning needed at this stage with QuickBooks and ten hours of a small business accountant, probably around tax time. Ditto for a payroll clerk. That work can be outsourced very easily to companies that specialize in this.

However, some types of employees may need to be on your payroll. The employees you hire for your company should be grouped into three simple areas:

- Marketing
- Operations
- Administration

Marketing sells the business's products and services. This work may require several people and an increasing number as sales grow. Operations, which provides the products and services being sold, also could require several people. An administrative person deals with everything that supports marketing and operations. Structuring your company this way keeps the entrepreneur focused on the most important aspect of the startup: sales. You don't have to worry about defining a human resources or legal group, because these functions can be easily outsourced. Do only what is necessary to support sales.

Hiring People

With so many people unemployed right now, it is easy to hire sales representatives by paying only through commissions. Hiring commission-only salespeople keeps costs down and allows you to bootstrap and reduce risk. This way, you will have to pay your employees only when they add to the bottom line.

We believe in offering much higher than normal commissions to get good salespeople. Depending on the industry, commissions can run from 1 percent to 50 percent, depending on the price and profit margin of the product. Offering a commission that is twice the standard in the industry you are operating in (you can learn this standard simply by interviewing potential employees who have worked in the industry) is a smart way to attract the best salespeople.

Sharing ownership can be a part of the package if you have a really good salesperson and don't want him or her to leave if a better offer comes down the pike. You can offer the salesperson a small percentage of the company in exchange for reaching sales targets. Obviously, an attorney would have to write the contract. Since the company would not be publicly traded on a stock exchange, there would have to be provisions for selling the ownership stake back to you, the owner, if the salesperson decided to leave the company. But an equity stake would be an incentive for the salesperson to work even harder, and as the company's profits grow, the stake would become even more valuable.

Hiring sounds easy enough. You think of the role—what needs to be accomplished and how—and then you find the right person.

However, there are several common mistakes to avoid when hiring. Jim and Doug made a fairly common error with their business: they hired almost everyone they knew. Big mistake! If there is a compelling reason to hire a friend or family member, then do so, but you don't want to give people jobs just to do them a favor or, worse, create a job just to fill it with friends and/or family. Creating a superfluous job is never a good idea, since it saps profits. Creating a job as a favor for a friend or family member is even worse, since emotion is then involved, making it more complicated to let people go if they don't meet expectations. These complications set up the real possibility of turning a longtime friend or relative into an overnight enemy.

Also, be forewarned that just because someone experienced success in another venture or in a larger business environment, it doesn't mean that that the person's success there will translate into success for your startup. We've seen a number of startups bring on people solely because the owner thinks their success is transferable. Stick to people and skills that are a fit for the company. Previous success is important; it just can't be the only reason for bringing someone on.

Success in a larger business or a corporate culture is achieved in a very different environment than that of a small business or startup. The typical environment of a large corporation is built around having plenty of resources, an office, generous compensation and benefits, structure, and built-in accountability. This is not applicable to the fast-paced and high-stress environment of an entrepreneurial small business or startup. When hiring employees, you need to make sure they understand the differences: fewer corporate benefits, yes, but in exchange, greater upside opportunities such as rapid advancement in the company, stock ownership, etc. You need to make sure prospective hires buy into the excitement and potential of a startup. If they are the type of employees who care only about leaving at 5:00 P.M. on the dot or having good food in the cafeteria, it's probably not a good fit.

An Advisory Board

A board of advisers is an informal board and is not legally attached to the company. It's a group of people who advise the entrepreneur based on holes in the team or to provide general advice. The advisory board can play a vital role in a business. The entrepreneur looks to the board to help identify the gaps and plug them. Advisers can also play an important role in hiring employees, particularly top management. You can even involve advisers in the employee interview process, getting their feedback as you make these crucial hiring decisions.

It is to the entrepreneur's discretion how to set up and implement the board. We find it an absolutely indispensable tool to complement any team and to provide that compelling and provocative element absolutely necessary to attract investors. You can find advisers who have hard evidence of success in specialties you may need in your business. You can approach potential advisers and ask whether they would care to be placed on the "board of advisers." If they agree, you now have a group of experts at your disposal.

As it is an informal board, there isn't necessarily a set of guidelines that govern when meetings take place or how compensation is structured. If you choose, you can formalize the meetings or compensation. You also have the option to treat members of the board as individual resources who can be called on when needed. The downside to formalizing your board is that you start treading upon people's busy schedules, which may push them out of the role. There are ways around that, however. Chris was once on a formal board of advisers for a bank in Florida. The bank held scheduled meetings using conference calls. This allowed the board members a lower commitment while preserving the bank's ability to tap their expertise. Or, as noted, you can set up your board of advisers in such a way that you meet or talk on an individual level.

Building Your Advisory Board

The first step in building the board of advisers is identifying the purpose of the advisers. Are you looking to fill gaps in the team? Are you looking for certain expertise in a market or just general advice on building the company? Once you have identified the need for the advisers, you can start to list people you feel would best provide the needed assistance. This step will take some research and networking. Don't limit yourself to just your network; look outside your network. Perhaps the best person to advise you on a particular matter is in another city. If so, don't worry; you can still put that person on the list. It's like building a fantasy baseball team.

The next step is the challenging one. You are going to contact the people on the list and sell them the idea of being on your board of advisers. Call the first person on the list. If you don't reach that person by phone, leave a brief voice mail, and then send an e-mail or contact the person on LinkedIn. Be persistent in calling back, but practice professional patience. Also, practice humility when building the initial relationship. You're seeking each person's time and help. If some people haven't responded to your phone calls or e-mails, don't worry about it. Don't call them out for their lack of response. These are busy people.

LESSON #31

When forming an advisory board, you might as well swing for the fences. Go after your dream list first. The hardest part is picking up the phone and giving it a shot. You have nothing to lose by aiming high, though.

Once you are able to reach people on the phone, ask if you may talk to them for five minutes. Keep it brief, and honor the five-minute limit. The goal is to hook people for your board of advisers. The people you'll want on the board will be successful people and will be very busy. Interestingly, if you get them talking about the story of their business, they will blow right past the five minutes. If they choose to talk, let them do it. Remember, your goal is to encourage them to be your adviser. Ultimately, you're looking to ask each person if he or she would mind being on a list of people you're seeking to advise you on problems you may run into. That's easier to do with people who just spent fifteen minutes telling you about themselves. Always say who the other people on the list are, even if you haven't called those people yet. Don't lie, but say, "I plan on asking these other people, too." If someone says no or doesn't display any interest, then repeat the same process with the next person. As you move through these steps, you'll end up with a group of people who will become an informal board of advisers, who will become champions for your business.

In putting together a dot-com startup for downtown merchants, Chris needed to build a board of advisers who had experience in working with small to medium-sized downtowns. He found a woman who was well known in government main street associations. She was arguably the best in her field. Chris called her and was able to reach her on the first try. He asked if he could have five minutes to speak with her about his business and then gave a brief description of it. Due to the connection of the business and her career, she had no problem with giving him some time.

He started by asking her a few questions about herself and her career, and immediately a connection was built. Toward the end of his five minutes, he asked her if she would allow him to put her on a list of people he could call on for advice and help. She not only said yes, but also asked to meet him for lunch to go over a few ideas. Jim created a board with a national magazine editor, an industry insider who converted two private companies into publicly traded ones, and several other industry stars.

As an entrepreneur, you should consider building an advisory board to be as important as hiring employees. It really does have the potential to grow your business by expanding connections and providing a base of wisdom and leadership to guide you as the company expands.

Building a board of advisers can be an intimidating process at first, and it takes diligence and legwork. If you have the energy and put forth the effort, though, you'll be able to assemble a group of people to help you build your business. What you'll quickly learn is that successful people love to help and give back. They have had mentors and others who assisted them on their path. You are giving them the opportunity to do the same. Being considerate of their time and inquisitive of their experience will go a long way to building a lasting relationship. It's like going to a grandmother and asking her for five minutes to describe her grandkids. She'll talk right past five minutes. This is similar for the entrepreneur.

The people you approach will say they are very busy and can only give you five minutes. Once you get them talking about their business, they'll talk to you for an hour. As you will learn very soon, for the entrepreneur, the business is very much his or her baby. In this process of building a board of advisers, it is always good to get people talking about their "baby." It cements the connection and increases the likelihood that they'll be interested in the business you're getting off the ground. A great board will help make your business compelling and provocative, and it will be something you can tout when you're attempting to lure top talent to come work for you.

11

Buying a Business and Franchising

THIS MAY SOUND TOO GOOD TO BE TRUE, but listen close: it is possible to buy an existing business with little or no money down. Your BS meter may have just gone off, and we hope it did—that means you are paying attention and that you're becoming skeptical, as any entrepreneur should be, of all offers that sound too good to be true. There are always thousands of businesses for sale; that's a given. You can check websites such as BizBuySell (http://www.bizbuysell.com) and find thousands of listings, some of which will no doubt be in your industry or area of expertise. These can be small, home-based businesses or medium-sized companies with offices, warehouses, and employees. However, the real question is whether it's possible to buy a business, one with existing revenue, for little or no money down.

The answer is yes.

No Money Down

Here is an example drawn from the personal experiences of one of the authors. Chris once purchased a janitorial service that had contracts at many large commercial buildings. He bought the company with no money down by agreeing to pay the owner a 20 percent royalty on all the existing contracts. His pitch to the owner went something like this: "I do all the work, saving you the headaches of running the business. You can sit at home and collect a check each month."

The owner knew that if Chris stopped paying, he could always take the business back. The risk for Chris also was low, since he did not have any of his own cash invested. If the business failed, Chris could simply hand the keys back to the owner. It was a great low-risk way to create a revenue stream. He did not borrow against his life savings. His health insurance was not at risk. Ultimately, Chris operated the company for a short time and sold it at a profit.

There are other ways to structure the financing so you can buy a business with no money. Many of these transactions, by necessity, require owner financing, since bank funding can be hard to obtain for small business purchases. Sellers know, or will learn very soon in the process, that they will be required to accept some form of owner financing. This means you can get control of a business for only a fraction of its list price. If you purchase a business through a business broker, it is common for the brokerage to seek a 30 percent down payment, with the buyer making payments on the balance over a period of five to seven years. And remember, if one business owner rejects your no-down-payment offer, don't be discouraged, because there are hundreds more owners out there, and you can pitch them with similar offers.

LESSON #32

Seller financing is the norm in today's market and is one key way to low-risk business purchasing.

The key with that type of transaction or any purchase with no money down is to win the trust and confidence of the owner, building a relationship. Invest several weeks with the owner/seller, and get to know both the individual and the business. Learn everything you can from him or her. One of our favorite tactics is to offer full asking price for the business. That may sound crazy, but it opens all sorts of new doors of opportunity. You are probably the only buyer the owner will ever have who has offered full asking price, and it puts the seller in the position of owing you a favor, perhaps by waiving any requirement for money up front.

While it starts with a handshake deal, you will still have to go through a contract signing. You should probably hire an attorney to write the contract, called an asset purchase agreement, which is usually very simple, only about ten pages or so. You might suggest that you and the seller split the attorney fee. With an asset purchase agreement, you are buying all the assets of the business, including the name and the inventory, but not the business itself. This means you will not be legally responsible for any lawsuits stemming from the previous owner's actions. But it also means that in addition to signing the sales contract, you will need to form a new corporation. The paperwork for incorporation also is very simple and can be done on any number of legal-document websites. You might also want to have the seller sign a noncompete agreement that will prevent him or her from setting up a duplicate business a few blocks away for a specified time period, say, two to five years. If you want the seller to stay on for a few months to train you in the new business, you would need him or her to sign an employment agreement as well.

Owner financing is a big reason purchasing a business with little or no money is possible. Banks will almost always require a significant down payment. Owners are usually much more flexible.

Advantages of Buying a Business

The business you decide on will already have existing sources of money flowing through it. You should plan to use these sources to fund the business purchase. Think of all of the potential in inventory, accounts receivable, accounts payable, and other assets. All of these resources can be creatively utilized in a deal structure. Take inventory, for example. According to a recent study, most businesses carry approximately 20 percent in excess inventory. Say a business owner wants a $50,000 down payment. You close on the sale and write the owner a $50,000 check, asking him or her not to cash it for two weeks, which the owner may be more willing to do if you are paying full asking price. During the first two weeks of owning the business, you liquidate the excess inventory. There are companies that will buy it in bulk from you on the spot, and you arrange it before you actually have control, so you can execute the second you sign the papers. You then have the funds to cover the check and your down payment.

Say the business you want to buy has several vehicles. You can get someone to purchase the vehicles from you—providing you the up-front cash needed to close the deal—and lease the vehicles back from the purchaser. The purchaser of the vehicles makes a healthy profit with no risk, as it is secured by the vehicles. Also, you get the benefit of up-front cash necessary to close. You free up cash for the down payment. Your only potential loss is the vehicles, not your life savings. Perhaps the company you are buying has a suitable location for a billboard or a cell phone tower, or maybe its parking lot could be sublet at night to a nearby nightclub. These are all ways you can tap cash up front to make a delayed down payment.

There are many other advantages of buying an existing business. You have immediate cash flow; that is, if you close on the sale at 3:00 P.M., the money that comes in at 4:00 P.M. belongs to you. That is not the case with a startup, which may take weeks or months to generate a sale. Also, the business you buy already has both customers and suppliers. It probably has a credit line with the suppliers or perhaps even a bank, which can further help cash flow and reduce the burden of your early marketing efforts. The seller typically provides training to the new owner. You will learn the business from an experienced person who has learned from his or her own mistakes. Since the seller does not want the business back, it is in his or her best interest to train you properly so that you will succeed.

Disadvantages of Buying a Business

There are also pitfalls in buying a business. Inevitably, even the most enticing of business purchases will have hidden problems. Problems will surface that you could not have anticipated. For instance, the culture of the business may be different from the one you wanted to create. When you look at a business, it is important to examine the culture ahead of time. Is it the kind of office where everybody works from home on Friday? Are there employees who have to leave at 4:00 P.M. each day regardless of the workload? You will inherit those employees, so make sure they will fit into your program. If you intend to be an ambitious, hard-charging entrepreneurial owner who is ready to take the company to a new level, you don't want to be stymied by an incompetent workforce.

You also need to determine as well as possible the reputation of the business you are buying, because you will automatically inherit that reputation. And you are buying somebody's problems. If the company has been ripping off customers for years, those disgruntled customers will be showing up at your doorstep, demanding satisfaction. Make sure the company you are buying is not conducting business in a way you feel is unethical. In some instances, unethical business practices might actually be the reason the company is profitable in the first place. If you eliminate the practice, you might suddenly find that you bought a money-losing business.

Potential pitfalls like these make it all the more imperative to have as little of your own cash in the business as possible. Less is better. Zero is the best of all.

Do Not Discount Franchising

Some entrepreneurs argue that franchising is not true entrepreneurship, as you didn't create the company from scratch. However, this can be a shortsighted view, particularly if your goal is making money. We become entrepreneurs to control our own futures, to generate multiple income streams, and to enjoy the freedom of setting our own schedules (also, of course, to make money!). Starting up with a franchise is a legitimate road to all of those destinations. In Chapter 3 on creativity, we told you to model your idea on successful businesses; franchising is basically an extension of that philosophy.

Owning a franchise does not make you any less of an entrepreneur. You still have to get out and drum up business. You are still responsible for delivering a satisfactory product to the customer. You still have to operate as efficiently as possible and keep your overhead to a minimum. There are, however, a few things working in your favor. Franchises have lower risks than other startup businesses, because the business model has been tested by hundreds of other franchisees, and the kinks are usually worked out. Also, the training, national advertising, and bulk-buying opportunities eliminate risks you would otherwise have to take alone.

Another factor working in your favor is that the franchisor does not want a franchise to fail. Failure hurts the company's reputation and reduces its revenue, since franchisees pay a percentage of their sales revenues to the franchisor. That is why a company will usually do whatever it can to prevent failure, including training the franchisee and ensuring that the store is located in the right place and the business is operated efficiently.

Buying a franchise also means that you immediately have hundreds of instant colleagues who also own franchises within the same company, all of them in the same boat, dealing with the same challenges, and working to help each other. Failure hurts the other franchisees as well, since it casts the brand in a negative light. If customers have a bad experience in one franchise, they are less likely to go to other stores in the same chain. The other franchisees, therefore, will back you up, and that support will be there from day one when you buy in.

LESSON #33

A good franchise will produce enough profit in the first year to cover the franchise fee.

Franchises can be quite lucrative. Chris owned a house-painting franchise. His students sometimes ask him why he paid $45,000 for a painting franchise when anybody can start a company to paint houses. He replies that yes, anybody can start a painting company, but how many people can start a painting company that does $700,000 in business in the first year with a 16 percent profit margin? That was Chris's experience. He not only recouped his franchise fee but also made a decent profit over and above that in the first year. When you buy a franchise, you are simply buying a system of doing business. It is usually a system that has been tested and proven by the franchisor, so less risk is associated with the investment.

One downside of franchises is that they can require a substantial amount of cash up front, to make the initial purchase, to get the business operating, and to cover operating expenses during the initial startup phase. Franchises are not necessarily the kind of business that can be easily bootstrapped, starting with little or no money and slowly building the company over time. We acknowledge that this places franchising outside our normal low-risk, bootstrapping model. This model is not right for everyone. That said, if you have been forced into early retirement and have a lump-sum settlement, you might want to consider a franchise.

You will be amazed at all the options. Several websites, such as Franchise Direct (http://www.franchisedirect.com), provide information about hundreds of franchise opportunities and include pricing information. There is literally a franchise opportunity available in every single American industry. Interestingly, you really don't have to be an expert in any particular field to buy a franchise. Chris did not know much about painting and had never been a painter, yet he ran a successful painting franchise. How would you like to own an emergency medical clinic with physicians as your employees? Franchises are available for those urgent-care centers, although they can require an up-front investment of around $500,000. You may have seen stores that advertise medical lab testing. Some of those franchises can be purchased for less than $30,000. There are franchises for drug testing, teeth whitening, weight loss, and dental equipment repair. The list goes on and on.

In addition to websites, there are numerous franchise trade shows, where you can talk to hundreds of franchisors at a single setting. Many offer financing options, but that might require you to put up collateral, such as your house or other assets. We, of course, would never approve of this. Keep looking.

Remember that the franchisors are selling you a product, so approach these presentations just as you would a car dealer or someone trying to sell you a timeshare. Be skeptical, and ask a lot of questions. One typical technique is for the franchise salesperson to pretend the franchisor is very selective about who the company will accept, that you must first make it through a screening process. Some franchisors are indeed selective; Chick-fil-A, for example, will screen applicants, perform background checks, and make sure applicants have adequate experience in operating a small business. But others will take almost anyone who has the available cash. Once you begin discussions with the company, don't be overly flattered if you are "accepted" for a franchise. Scarcity creates demand, and the company may simply be trying to make you think this is a great honor, when in fact your real asset is the $50,000 settlement check you got from your previous employer when you were laid off.

Considerations Before Buying into a Franchise

Perhaps the most vital thing to do before you buy a franchise is talk to other franchisees on your own, away from the salesperson. Visit the franchise locations, ask the franchisees about their cash flow and profit margins, and ask frank questions about the parent company and how it treats franchisees. Does the company impose unreasonable conditions on franchisees so it is hard to make a profit, such as requiring franchisees to buy ingredients from the parent company at inflated prices? Is the national advertising effective? Try to get to the real backstory, not the fluff in the franchise brochures.

Be wary, too, of franchise brokers. These are freelance salespeople who represent lots of companies, much as a mortgage broker does. Some might even conduct a personality profile on you and make it appear that they are coming up with a perfect match. They will come back with a list of franchises that are supposedly the most suitable for you, and only you. But what really motivates these brokers is the commission they get from the sale. If they get a $15,000 commission from one sale and $30,000 from another, which do you think they will try to sell you? Another problem with brokers is that they work for companies that have to hire people to sell the franchises. Brokers therefore would be more likely to push obscure franchises that are harder to sell. A popular, big-name franchisor doesn't need to hire a broker.

It's extremely important to read the franchise agreement thoroughly before you sign and to hire a franchise lawyer to go over it with you. Many of the contracts are standard; they apply to every franchisee and can't be changed. But they can reveal aspects of the deal that may be unappealing, and you should know in advance what you are signing.

Franchisors make much of their money by charging you a royalty on sales, but some also profit from forcing you to buy all your ingredients and supplies from them, instead of buying on the open market, where the same items might be of better quality and less expensive. This is understandable if, for example, it's the restaurant's secret sauce, a unique product that you can find nowhere else. You want to avoid having to buy routine products from the parent company. Make sure the purchasing requirements aren't too onerous. Also, make sure you can transfer the franchise to someone else, without fee, if you decide to sell.

If you decide to buy a franchise, remember that it is just like any other business: you have to build it. Yes, you get your initial two weeks of training, a manual, an occasional phone call from the front office, and the annual franchisee convention. But no matter how well the company supports you, it's still your business at the end of the day, and you've got to build it. For some reason, that lesson is lost on some people. They buy the franchise and expect the business to thrive magically because of company support, not because of their own efforts. They complain that the company is not doing anything to help. The parent company will help you with marketing, but it won't do the marketing for you. You have to do that yourself. The franchisor will give advice on how to run the company, but it won't run the franchise for you. Only one person will ensure that the business, whether it is a franchise or something else, is ultimately successful: you!

12

Knowing What Your Business Is Worth

ONCE YOUR BUSINESS APPEARS TO BE FUNCTIONING at or around the level you were striving for, it's important to take the time to calculate exactly where you stand financially. In this chapter, we will be introducing you to the concept of valuation—knowing what your business is worth and, more importantly, how to maximize that value.

Understanding what a business is worth, or its value, is an elusive goal. This is a place where many entrepreneurs and business owners make several mistakes. First, many people will overestimate the value of the business. The business is yours, so you think it is worth more than it really is. Second, many business owners don't really know what drives value in a business and, thus, don't know how to focus on it. The danger here is that if you've not paid attention to the value of your business, then you will end up damaging your net worth. Therefore, even if you are just starting, this information is critical. In this chapter, we are going to talk about the value within a startup business. We will look at the difference between price and value, and summarize the formal valuation process.

A Quick Warning

If you follow the advice of this book to the letter, you will not fall into the trap of having to rely on raising capital from outside sources. But if you raise outside capital anyway, we consider it our duty to inform you that your business may not be worth much to you when you sell it. If you start your business with someone else's money, that someone owns a piece of your company and profits—sometimes a big piece. When you sell, the investors get a large portion of your money. If you start the business slowly with your own money, you will be able to keep more of your profits when sales increase, making your business even more valuable to you when you decide to sell.

The Difference Between Value and Price

Jim and Chris each have had experience with business valuations and appraisals. Chris started and ran a business valuation venture, while Jim, through his experience with his education company, dealt with appraisals and their impact on fund-raising, restructuring, and selling a business. Jim's experience has been that the appraisal almost always comes in lower than the owner expects. Chris has found that this is a common reaction of business owners who have put years of sweat equity into their business and often think it is worth more than it really is. That is why an appraisal, although not always perfect, can be a valuable exercise for a business owner, who may not always be totally objective about the business value, much as parents don't always see the flaws in their own children.

Do you know the difference between the value and the price of a business? In describing a business, value and price are two different things and often are not equal. Let's quickly define price. Price occurs at the intersection of the demand and supply curves; it's what one will pay for something, given the supply and demand for that item. Value is the inherent worth of something as defined by one person. Value changes from person to person, so it is subjective. When people ask what their business is worth, they are making a mistake. It is the wrong question to ask. Instead, the business owner needs to increase the value of the business in the eyes of a potential purchaser. Doing so ultimately increases its price. Remember, value changes based on who is ascertaining the value.

LESSON #34

Value and price are not equal. Value is the inherent worth. Price is what someone will really pay for it.

A business's value, like beauty, is in the eye of the beholder. One person could look at something and find beauty in it, while another sees absolutely nothing. Part of what value experts do is try to create objective standards to define value, hoping to normalize price. This ends up being fruitless for the entrepreneur, because a buyer could potentially place a higher value on a business than the appraiser did. For example, if you own a house, then you clearly understand the difference between value and price. Many homeowners who purchased in the early 2000s have a sharply different view of the value of their homes than do would-be homeowners currently looking to purchase. To the first group, their house is worth, say, $250,000—

the value they assign based on the price they once paid. Today's market may inform the second group that the correct price is actually $200,000. For another example, let's say you have an old watch from your grandfather. While the watch might be able to fetch only $30 on eBay, to you, this watch has an inherent value that is much higher. This difference between value and price speaks to the complexity of valuation.

Additionally, there can be a very inconsistent relationship between profitability, sales, and value. A business can be both growing and profitable but have no value besides the physical assets. We once knew two business owners who started a very successful staffing agency. They ran this business successfully for a number of years, achieving healthy revenues in a sustainable business. What surprised us was that when they decided to transition out of the business, they simply closed the doors, sold off any physical assets, and moved on. The founders had created the business's value, and if they left, then the company could not be purchased. What they could have done but did not do was train other people to operate the company. Then the business could have been sold as a going concern and would have continued to operate smoothly under new owners. That would have given the business real value beyond the mere physical assets.

Conversely, is it possible for a business to be unprofitable yet immensely valuable? It sounds highly illogical, but it is possible. Think of the dot-com days. Companies were created with very intriguing ideas, very little infrastructure, and no sales. They were then sold at ridiculously high prices, based on expectations of great growth in the future. Many of these companies later flopped, not living up to expectations. Others, such as Amazon.com, are flourishing. Even today, there are very similar examples in Twitter and Facebook. Both of these companies have much higher inherent value than their current profits would suggest.

You now see the challenge to ascertaining value, which leads to discrepancies between a business's price and its value.

Valuation Companies

Business appraisers or valuation companies essentially take this tension and try to create objective standards by which to value companies. There's an entire formalized industry and a set of standards by which appraisers determine a business's value. The first important thing to know is that the appraiser, through the written appraisal report, is really just offering an opinion of value. At the end of the day, the appraiser's opinion of value is his or her subjective opinion, and even though it is based on analyses and solid information, it is still an opinion. For example, how much are a company's reputation and goodwill in the community worth? A really popular brand that is widely known in a city or state has an intrinsic value that may be hard to quantify. A product may be unique, so there is little for an appraiser to compare it with; consequently, the appraiser simply makes a guess.

Second, it's important to know that appraisals or valuations are often done for particular reasons, not just to answer a business owner's curiosity. Primarily, business valuations and/or appraisals are used for partnership disputes and for estate and gift taxes, issues that are unlikely to affect a budding entrepreneur. But once your business is a strong going concern, you may at some point need to get an appraisal. You may also need an appraisal of a business you are trying to purchase.

Appraisers predominantly use the fair market value standard. This is a standard that sets the guidelines and procedures for assigning value. It is used in the majority of valuations. Due to some of the technical aspects, this valuation standard typically provides a lower value than others, and it is usually lower than what the business owner might like to see. Knowing this can be helpful if you want to purchase a business and if you are considering bringing in an appraiser to provide an opinion of value that will help determine the price of the purchase.

The Three Approaches to Valuation

There are three primary approaches to valuation. First, the asset approach values the company based on the physical assets of the company, such as the building it is in, equipment such as machinery and trucks, inventory, and cash in the bank. From the value of these assets, the appraiser subtracts liabilities such as loans on the assets, unpaid taxes, and judgments in lawsuits. Second, the income approach uses financial analysis and reporting to arrive, basically, at an annual amount of money the business brings in, relative to expenses. Third, the market-based approach takes into account what someone will actually pay for the business. Of the three, the income approach is used most often.

General economic conditions also are considered in a valuation or appraisal report. In better economic times, values for certain business will be higher, and vice versa. Some accountants tend to focus only on the past, though. They want five years' worth of previous financials statements that they will use as a basis for forecasting future sales and estimating value.

This is only part of the equation; many other elements must be considered. The particular industry, for instance, also is important. If one were valuing an American auto parts supplier two years ago, the state of the auto industry and the abysmal forecast for the auto industry would have lowered estimates of value. It is important to note that the appraiser's opinions on the industry's growth potential could vary from appraiser to appraiser.

LESSON #35

You should be able to repay the purchase price in three years, using the business's cash flow.

Maximizing the Value of Your Business

Given that normally 60 to 80 percent of an entrepreneur's net worth is tied to his or her business, it's natural to want to know how much the business is worth. However, this is the wrong question for an entrepreneur to ask. The right question is, "How do I maximize the value of my business so that I can sell my business for the highest amount?"

We hope your business is successful enough that one day you will be pondering its value as you plan on eventually selling it or passing it down to your children. Or you may be fortunate enough to find a good business to buy and need to know its real value. When those situations arrive, you will probably learn more than you ever wanted to know about business evaluations. We hope this chapter gives you a glimpse of what they may entail.

13

When Can I Quit My Day Job?

IDEALLY, YOU WILL BE GAINFULLY EMPLOYED while you launch your new business venture, running your new firm after work and on weekends, and perhaps even using some vacation days to grow sales. We have described in this book a general process for finding your business idea and told you it is OK to borrow an idea if you don't have one of your own. We suggested you invest less than $10,000 to start your business—or at least no more than you can afford to lose. We got you to think about starting internationally, drop shipping, and buying an existing business or a franchise. Certainly, you will be using the Internet every step of the way to get your product or service in front of as many eyeballs as possible.

By the end of your first quarter, you should have had a couple thousand in sales. By the end of the first year, you should have revenue of at least $10,000, having learned a lot. Now what? Repeat? Grow? But what about health insurance? If your business succeeds, and we firmly believe that it will, with minimal risks, you ultimately will face the option of leaving your day job and plunging full-time into entrepreneurship.

It is a tempting choice but one that should not be made lightly. Working for a company, particularly if the job comes complete with health insurance and other benefits, can anchor a person. Our jobs define us. Having somewhere to go, someone to report to, someone to gossip with, and tasks to do are important. One of the revelations that seems to surprise many new entrepreneurs is how much they miss the idle chat at the copy machine, the dreaded Christmas party, and, of course, the benefits of their old job.

No matter how cushy your day job is, you may find yourself spending forty hours a week working at it and thirty hours a week working on your business. This balance will work for an indefinite period, but what happens when you want to expand the business even further? After all, doing so would probably require at least another thirty hours of work a week. There simply aren't enough hours in the day.

One day, it will be time to make a choice.

Benefits of Keeping Your Job

During your first year, you learned so many things. You had plenty of successes, but you also made so many mistakes that you wish you could do it all over again differently. However, you are still alive and kicking, and you have lots of ideas on how to grow. In your second year, your business may earn $100,000, bringing in some real profit. You still have your job, but it is really straining your marriage and killing your free time, and you haven't seen a movie in forever. By the time year three rolls around, it will be very hard to keep both the job and business.

The job gives you the stability to run the business without worrying about salary for yourself as owner. Profit can be reinvested to grow the company. This gives you a distinct advantage—perhaps more of an advantage than the extra time would represent, if you resigned. Before quitting your day job, you might want to consider hiring someone to work that extra thirty hours needed to grow your business. If you make $40 an hour at your day job and have health insurance, hiring someone at $20 an hour with no benefits may make more sense than quitting—but only if your profit margins are enough to justify the salary expense. The smart goal in that case would be to hire a reliable full-time employee who would completely manage your business, under your supervision. But remember that it takes time to develop a company with enough profit to cover a manager and still put money into your own bank account. Only consider hiring a manager when your profits are more than enough to cover the salary of a manager you would be lucky to get.

A manager making an average salary with no benefits is not likely to be as motivated. An incentive system that allows the manager to get a bonus based on profits is a good idea. It turns the manager into an entrepreneur. You might also consider giving the manager stock in the company as a bonus. Our bar owner Joey Tatum has profit sharing for every employee.

Hiring a manager not only allows you to keep your day job, with its retirement, health insurance, and salary, it also creates the chance for you to grow or to launch other businesses.

Benefits of Multiple Businesses

Having more than one business is the ultimate low-risk strategy. Just as you would not want to put your entire retirement fund into one stock, you would not want to have one business if there is opportunity to have several. Every new business is a new revenue stream that reduces risks and makes your family safer. Even if you work for a great company like Microsoft, you still have more risk than if you own three small businesses. Having multiple businesses also gives you greater options when considering when or if to quit your day job. With more money coming in and your risk diversified, you should be in a much better position to quit the day job if that is what you choose to do. Or you can use the revenue from several businesses to hire managers for your businesses. Either way, you have more options, more freedom.

Starting a second and third business will be much easier than launching the first. By the time you start a second business, you will have already learned from the first business how to do the basics— how to keep overhead low, how to avoid risky strategies, and how to build slowly and sustainably. When you start an additional business, the basic rules are the same, even though the product or service may be different.

What seems to work best, and what you should strive to do if possible, is to have companies that complement each other. For example, if you sell high-end binoculars for bird-watchers, you could also sell books on birds or any other product that would appeal to that group of customers. Since you are already targeting that audience, your marketing efforts will already be poised for success. At that point, it's simply a matter of cross-referencing each business in ads, fliers, e-mails, and websites.

LESSON #36

When starting an additional business, strive to pick one that complements your initial business. Doing so will make your marketing efforts go twice as far.

Look for businesses that can be accommodated in the same warehouse space and that use the same packing materials. You might also look for business ideas that run countercyclical to your other products. If you have items that sell well at Christmas, pick another product that does well in the spring or fall. This way, you will always have a business opportunity at the ready. One of the great advantages of having multiple businesses is that it allows for year-round cash flow. When one business is in a slump, the others pick up the slack.

Remember, you are not a slave to your day job. If you follow the advice in this book, it is entirely possible that you will soon have several thriving businesses to your credit. Having three or four profitable businesses means being able to walk away from the corporate grind if need be. Just knowing that will make your day job more tolerable. You will be emotionally and financially invulnerable to downsizings, transfers, demotions, and salary cuts. Additionally, the management skills you learn as an entrepreneur will likely improve your performance at the day job, which could lead to a promotion—*if* you decide to continue working there.

It is important, too, not to be a slave to health insurance. Many people are afraid to leave their day jobs, because by doing so they will lose company-subsidized health insurance. But if leaving your day job means doubling your salary from $40,000 a year to $80,000 a year, then a $1,000 a month health insurance bill should not get in your way. That corporate health insurance would, in effect, be costing you $28,000 a year or more if it blocked you from becoming a successful entrepreneur. Also, when you are a small business owner, the premiums you pay when purchasing your own health insurance can be tax deductible. For those with preexisting conditions, the 2010 Patient Protection and Affordable Care Act created high-risk pools at the state level, meaning you will get coverage somewhere. Premiums can be high and coverage low, but there is coverage available. In 2014, you will be able to buy coverage through health insurance exchanges, which are designed to be affordable to individuals and small businesses. For more information, go to the federal government's HealthCare.gov website (http://www.healthcare.gov).

LESSON #37

For a small business owner, the premiums paid when purchasing health insurance can be tax deductible. More information is available at HealthCare.gov.

Anyone who claims to know what health care is going to look like in two or three years is lying, of course. Here is our favorite strategy that is available to you right now. Many Chambers of Commerce, especially medium-sized Chambers, allow their members to join a larger pooled plan for health insurance. Any business owner can join the local Chamber of Commerce. Join the right Chamber, and you might find an affordable health care plan.

The bottom line is that you have many choices, options, and opportunities. And you control these choices. Being an entrepreneur gives you more choices.

What Happens When You Call It a Day

It's only when you are ready to sell off your businesses or start a completely new career that the payoff of your hard work really starts to come through in a way that can't be replicated in the corporate world. At this point, you can sell your business (or just one of your businesses if you have multiple business), most likely for many, many times more than you invested initially. On the opposite end of the spectrum, you can't sell your job when you leave a corporation.

When you eventually cash out of your company, you will have the freedom to do many things—travel, help other entrepreneurs get started by investing in their companies, engage in philanthropy, sleep. The list is long. You should be thinking about this now, even in the early days of your business, even when retirement is decades away. You should incorporate your retirement strategy into the way you run the company as you are building it. Don't wait until the very end, when it may be too late.

After all, you're definitely going to get out of your business one day, whether as a result of retirement, death, divorce, disability, or other factors. You should plan for these contingencies early on. It's important for an entrepreneur to have life and disability insurance, a will, and a plan for the business after you've moved on. Will you simply shut it down and sell the excess inventory in a going-out-of-business sale? That is certainly an option, and it's one of the advantages of owning your own business. You can simply switch it off whenever you want and walk away, although there are, of course, issues that come with that. For one thing, there are your employees. You do not want to leave employees out in the lurch after years of loyal service. But if you plan for this, you can give them plenty of notice so they can prepare for the closing of the business. Barring extenuating circumstances, you should give your employees at least two years' notice of your pending retirement—even more if you can.

You may want to pass the business on to your children, but that comes with another set of issues. Your children may not be at all interested in taking it over. Perhaps your son or daughter is a brain surgeon in Manhattan and has no time or inclination to sell widgets from China. Maybe only one of your three children wants the business. In fairness, the other two probably deserve shares in the company as passive partners. How do you arrange that? It is not something you want to do on the fly and may take years of planning with a financial expert.

Maybe a loyal employee wants to buy the business. This option is ideal, because the person will know the business inside and out, and you'll be more or less keeping it in the "family." But how will that employee come up with the money to buy a business overnight?

(At that point, your business will hopefully be worth millions of dollars.) The answer is planning. If you have identified the challenge years ahead of time, you can create a financial plan that enables the employee to assume control when you leave. This might include giving the employee stock in the company as a bonus each year, so when your retirement approaches, the employee already owns a big share of the company. You could finance the remainder of the sale, and the employee could make payments out of the profits of the business.

This brings us back to the subject of valuation. As you are planning for retirement and deciding how much money you will need to live comfortably, the value of your business is a key factor. How much are you going to get out of it at the end? Again, this is a factor you should be thinking about years ahead of time, so you can either build the business's value as close to that amount as possible or sock away enough cash from the profits that you can simply shut down your company and walk away. These are all decisions that, as a successful entrepreneur, you will one day have to face.

Succession Planning

An interesting question to consider is this: can the company function without you? Are you the kind of business owner who hasn't taken a vacation in five years because you fear that if you did, sheer chaos would result? If so, your business may have no real value when you leave. You are the business, and that means the company is one heartbeat away from being worthless. If that's the case, then it will also be worthless once you decide to retire.

To cash in on your business at the end of your career, you need a strategy that will slowly extricate you from the day-to-day operations of the company. You need to create a system that sustains the business regardless of whether you are there and regardless of whether your long-term manager with twenty years of experience is there.

That is why succession planning is so important to a big corporation. There is a system in place that creates a steady supply of managers who are trained and can easily run the company at a moment's notice. Not all of them will be the CEO, but there is a pipeline of people who are capable of taking over the top job. This is true for small businesses as well. If the manager of a McDonald's restaurant keels over from a heart attack, does the store close the next day? Of course not. The burgers and fries keep flowing off the assembly line.

That is how a sustainable business must operate. But that takes a system that has to be developed and refined over years. You should try as much as possible to incorporate that kind of strategy into your business from day one. It can actually make owning a business more fun. As the business grows and becomes more profitable, you are slowly disengaging, delegating responsibility as the company becomes a self-sustaining concern, giving you more free time, more time to relax.

If you follow a succession plan, the demands on your time will gradually decrease by a large margin. As retirement approaches, you will be working fifteen hours a week instead of eighty. There will be time for the grandchildren, golf, travel, puttering around in the garden, relaxing, reducing stress, improving your health.

A good way to test whether you are effectively winding down your involvement in the business is to plan a vacation smack in the middle of your company's busiest time of year. If you return to find chaos, then you need to work harder on your exit strategy. If you arrive back at work and find that the company never even missed you, then you are on the right track.

If you have a fully functioning tight ship, imagine how much more valuable the company will be to potential buyers. You can take them on a tour of the company and point out that it runs ahead at full steam without you. That gives the company real value because the buyer is purchasing not you, but the business you created. You are retiring and won't be around anymore, but your operation will survive. The buyer wants a company that can survive and thrive on its own.

If your company has evolved into the kind that can run on its own without you, it is time to take the big payoff check, sit back, and enjoy the rewards of your hard work. You were the one who years before believed in yourself and in the power of free enterprise, left the corporate world, and decided to create your own destiny. Now that destiny is here.

Enjoy it. You earned it.

Conclusion

Determination Is Everything

THE SINGLE MOST IMPORTANT THING to remember is that you can do this. If you've stuck with us this far, you are fully capable of starting a business that will change your life. Hopefully, the stories of all the regular people you've met in this book will provide you with the examples needed for taking the first step in changing your life. It's as simple as finding an idea that will work in your community and improving on it. Build slowly from a small base, remembering to never get ahead of your cash flow and to fight every expense. Remember that there's a limitless supply of people and resources to help and guide you along your way.

You should also remember that we will be there to help you as well. Sign on to The Entrepreneur School website (http://www.the entrepreneurschool.com) now for a wealth of additional tools that will help you along the way.

To wrap things up, we would like to introduce you to Tierra Reid, a young mother of two who had a corporate job but felt a pull toward something more that was impossible to ignore. Her story integrates many of the lessons we've discussed over the course of this book, so it is only fitting to include it here at the end. Here it is, in her words:

Many people say they want something, when it turns out they're not ready to do even half of what it takes to give it a true shot. People sometimes tell me that I'm so lucky. I don't quite understand how what I did could be interpreted as luck. If by "luck," they mean making the conscious decision to take a big chance, asking for help when needed, going several nights without sleep, replacing "fun" things to do with strategic business planning and sacrificing, and investing every dime in a dream—if all that can be considered luck, then I guess I got really lucky.

Since I opened my first brick-and-mortar boutique, Stylish Consignments, in Lilburn, Georgia, last fall, an extraordinary amount of women have told me how lucky I am. Some go on to complain about the surplus of bills that they have, or the lack of spare time. The word if gets thrown around a lot, as in "if only I had waited to have children" or "if only I had more money." Other times, I hear, "If I only had a husband to help me" or "If I just had the contacts that you have."

I end up having to explain that I was not handed this business—I earned it. I'm growing it myself with seeds I planted. It was a conscious decision I made when I felt the timing was right.

I've had an entrepreneurial spirit since I was a child. My parents were my initial "investors." They went to Sam's Club and purchased candy for me. I soon discovered that the neighborhood kids would pay double for the convenience of buying candy anytime they wanted it. And I could also enjoy all the candy I wanted. We had a back patio with a window and screen that slid from side to side. I turned it into the perfect little shop, even going so far as to tape a price list to the window.

With that first little business venture, I learned a few early lessons. If you eat your stock, you might not profit or even break even. Sometimes I invested in candy that nobody wanted to buy. And since I didn't take the time to do a regular inventory, it took months for me to discover that my little sister was sneaking bubble gum! Selling candy was fun, but I quickly learned that there was more to it than I originally imagined.

By the time I was able to get a "real" job, I had reached a genuine milestone—getting a paycheck with my name on it! It felt great at fifteen and even better at twenty, when the value of a dollar started to mean so much more. I was hit with real-world concerns of student loans, books, housing—basically all the mess of life. My love for fashion led me to start a gift basket company, Gift Creations. I headed downtown to get a business license and started to understand the basic logistics of how it all tied together. I asked tons of questions, spent hours shopping for the materials, made a few prototypes, and began to take preorders. When I was not in class, I spent my nights and days making these beautiful baskets. I created my first set of business cards. Boy, did I feel special! I was official now!

I paid a friend to sell these gift baskets on commission, and she hooked me up with a barbershop so men could order them for their wives. I also paid the barbers to help me spray-paint fifty baskets at a time. I gave the shop owner free baskets for his wife, which accounted for my booth rent. It was a home run! I had started a small business while I was in college. However, I still worked part-time at a local department store to support myself. It seems I was not taking into account the value of my time, my gas, and the other variable expenses one might forget to think about. I discovered that I still needed hands-on business training.

I graduated from college with a degree in fashion merchandising and landed a corporate job working in the Macy's buying office. I was finally able to earn a real salary with benefits in the field I loved—fashion. It was another dream come true. I started a family with my very supportive husband. Together with my corporate job, they provided me with that sense of stability and security we all hope for in life. I felt truly blessed to have reached my goals of working in the fashion industry and also starting a family, but deep down inside, I still wanted more. I wanted to be in business for myself.

In my corporate career, I met a lot of great people who blew my mind with their talent. I sat in on meetings and business deals, and I began to understand how a large business operates successfully. I soaked up all of this knowledge and knew I was ready for more responsibility. Eagerly, I asked for a promotion time and time again, but the company couldn't keep up with my ambitions. I knew it was time to branch out.

Well, guess what happened next? My urge to branch out on my own was pushed even further when my company announced a mass layoff while I was on maternity leave with my second child. Everyone was scared—we were in the middle of a recession—but I knew that this was my chance to give my dream of owning my own business a shot. I had everything to lose, but I knew I had to take my shot or I would regret it.

I immediately started looking for information on how I could get started, and that's how I found the Small Business Administration website and The Entrepreneur School. I reconnected with my college alma mater to see what resources it provided for alumni who wanted to start their own businesses. My husband and I took several courses together, stayed up countless nights to develop a solid plan, and researched the business model that was right for me. We decided on a consignment clothing store that allows customers with new or nearly new clothing to sell unwanted items through our store. We would collect a commission on each sale.

As I worked on starting the store, I quickly found out that you work much harder for yourself than you ever will for anyone else. You will not let yourself down as others may. If you don't have an answer, you find it, especially when your livelihood is on the line. I became extremely focused on my leap of faith and doing whatever it took to make it a success.

As soon as I realized that the best possible version of my business would require a storefront, I purchased fixtures on Craigslist from a going-out-of-business sale. I bought the whole lot for $500 and then resold the unneeded items that came with it later on. I estimated that the store fixtures alone were worth over $3,000, so all in all, it was a great deal, and it reduced my up-front costs dramatically.

I rode around for hours and must have called dozens of Realtors, looking for just the right commercial space for my shop. I also met a developer who owned several shopping plazas. We connected instantly. While I couldn't afford any of the available space he was offering, he gave me the advice I needed to keep going. He said to picture the search as if I were combing through the clearance rack at Macy's: if you look hard enough and long enough, you will find the deal you want. Since he was a multimil-lionaire with twenty-five years of experience, I felt good about following his advice.

When I found the space I wanted, I sent him my lease to look over. We rewrote it to match my wish list and what was realistic for my budget. When I signed the lease and received the keys to my new store, I was so excited. I even managed to score a couple of months of free rent in the deal. I never knew anyone would agree to something like that, but these are the kind of things you find out in a negotiation. But what I learned is that all of the fear, procrastination, and false assumptions we have can hurt us. If you just go for it, things have a way of working out.

Looking back, the only thing I would do differently is set up the store quicker. We spent several months trying to get the store ready for our grand opening. Of course, I wanted everything to be perfect. Industry experts actually advise three to four weeks maximum, because you want to start making money before the rent kicks in. During that time, however, I acquired inventory on consignment from a failed store so that my boutique would open fully stocked. I bought a URL, had a website built, began marketing online, and planned a grand-opening party with local celebri-ties to attract media attention. In total, getting started cost about $6,000. That figure included my security deposit, fixtures, utilities, build-out, and software.

I can honestly say that starting my own store has been the most fulfill-ing business decision that I have ever made. The store has been open for eighteen months and is making a profit. For the first year, I plowed all the profits back into the business, but now I am actually on the payroll, writ-ing myself a check each month. The sleepless nights, the days when you are almost overwhelmed because you don't know what to do next, the hours that you spend isolated—all of these things were well worth it.

I don't refer to my decision to pursue entrepreneurship as luck; it is and always has been a conscious decision to work hard and take risks. I make mistakes and learn from them—and I have to learn quickly. I ask a lot of questions. I stay surrounded by motivating people who also put action behind their dreams, and I constantly tell myself that taking it slow will allow me to be there for my family and enjoy the journey along the way. When other women tell me they want to do what I did, but they are afraid, I remind them that every successful corporation began with someone making a brave decision to give him- or herself a shot. And you know what? So can you.

Appendix

Low-Risk Businesses
You Can Start Today

THERE IS AN ENDLESS LIST of businesses that can be started quickly and profitably. This chapter includes a few ideas from the authors for you to use as a starting point.

Baby Furniture Rental

One of our favorite ideas is to rent baby furniture. Many websites today rent items that a few years ago no one would have conceived of as a rental product. Now you can rent shoes, handbags, and even dresses off the Internet. It's a wide-open field.

Renting baby furniture to parents of newborns makes perfect sense. The furniture required for a newborn, such as cribs, rocking chairs, and changing stations, is only used for a very short time frame—perhaps less than one year. After that point, parents have to sell the baby items on Craigslist or give them away to another pregnant friend. Car seats, strollers, and many other short-lived items also can be available for rental. After one family has used the item for the necessary amount of time, the crib could be refurbished and rented to another family for their new baby. It is even possible to rent out baby clothing as well. The clothing the children wear from zero to three months is certainly not worn out after one baby, and it could easily be used again and again.

Green Products

There are environmental trade shows throughout the United States and throughout the world, with booth after booth of companies seeking distributors for products designed to save energy, reduce waste, and lower damage to the environment. One large environmental trade show is Americana, which is held in Montreal every two years, and there are many others that may be valuable for you to attend.

You can become a distributor for these products at fairly low cost and low risk. Many of them also save money for the purchaser in the long term. For example, there are companies that sell restaurants systems that trap grease in filters that are biodegradable and can be thrown away in regular garbage. Using these items saves money for restaurants by reducing the frequency with which they have to clean their grease traps. It can also help water quality by sending less grease into the sewer system.

Hundreds of these types of products are available, and you can find them fairly easily if you look online.

Recipe Kiosk

Imagine that in the front of every grocery store is a kiosk that helps you with your shopping and meal planning. The kiosk would offer thousands of recipes in many categories, sortable by the number of calories, the nutrient content, ingredients, price, or any other characteristic. Select a category, and the kiosk will dispense a printout of the recipes available in that category. Choose a recipe, and the ingredient shopping list appears on a printout. Grocery stores would pay a monthly fee for the kiosk, and the store could include product coupons and advertisements on the printout.

Social Network for Ride Sharing

Social networking sites like Facebook are incredibly popular, with hundreds of millions of people participating in them. A website that integrated some aspect of social networking with the useful function of arranging carpooling for people headed in the same direction would benefit a lot of people. Thousands drive the same commute every day, not knowing whether someone else is making the exact same trip. This is a waste of fuel, it makes the roads more crowded, and it slows traffic down. Imagine a website that allows you to input your favorite music and other personal information and then helps you arrange a carpool with like-minded passengers. You could charge a fee for this service or go for sponsorship dollars from environmental groups and local communities, perhaps even your local department of transportation.

Foreclosed-Property Management

With the increasing number of foreclosed homes, banks are now forced to sit on thousands and thousands of properties. Fortunately, many laws require that the banks maintain the properties so that neighborhood market values do not suffer. The banks must keep the lawns mowed, maintain the appearance of the houses, and do anything else necessary to prevent them from damage. This also includes timely visits inside the home to ensure that there is no damage from burst pipes or break-ins.

Banks are simply not designed to perform these services. You can easily establish a foreclosed-property management company by going to a bank and saying you will perform these required services for a small monthly fee per house. We love this business because it has virtually no startup fee, requires no special expertise, and is in a large growth area that should prosper for several years to come.

Moonlight Kitchen

Restaurants routinely toss perfectly good food at closing time. Establish a website that allows restaurants to sell food late at night for deep discounts, takeout only, with the restaurant updating its listings an hour or two before closing. Perhaps there is lasagna left over that a hungry user of the website can buy for half price at 10:00 P.M. The restaurant pays you a 15 percent commission plus a monthly base fee of, say, $45. Your job is to build and maintain the website, sign up restaurants, market the site, and train restaurant employees in how to upload their daily offerings.

Online Tutoring from India

The slumping economy will help an online tutoring company in very distinct ways. First of all, many unemployed and underemployed workers see the need for continuing education in technology and many other fields. Second, by using tutors based in India, the company will be able to substantially reduce costs. Tutoring companies could be started in many different specialties, teaching almost any skill set. Using videoconferencing technology such as Skype, the cost to build an online tutoring website could be very cheap. Using websites like oDesk and Elance, you can identify available Indian tutors quickly. This new-business idea actually holds the potential for several new companies, since there are so many different possible niches to focus on.

Ads for College Notebooks

College students go through notebooks by the dozen each semester. It would be easy to find an advertiser to sponsor some notebooks, which you would distribute free of charge to students, saturating campuses with the advertiser's message and at the same time helping students save money.

Anything, Anytime Delivery for Hotels

A great hotel will have the item you forgot to pack when you were at home. It will have the toothpaste or brush you are missing and will quickly bring it to you for a very small charge. However, what if you forget a more substantial item like a black belt or your size-nine loafers? In this business proposal, we suggest starting a company that caters to what the hotel does not have immediately available. You would run into any store in town and buy whatever is needed and immediately deliver it to any hotel in town. Within thirty minutes, you could have any item replaced, be it a specialty face cream or favorite college jersey. Again, such a business would require almost no startup capital and therefore has very little risks. It would be easy to start by simply going to every concierge in town and letting each one know that the service exists.

Hospital Spa Services

Another business plan that we simply love is to provide in-hospital spa services, because such a business is easy to start up, costs no money to get going, and serves a great niche. Today the norm is to take flowers along when visiting a hospital patient. But imagine instead that the patient gets a back rub, foot massage, or manicure instead of just receiving flowers. Hospital patients would appreciate it much more. Starting this business would be easy, quick, and inexpensive. Marketing could be done through the hospital itself. For example, the packages could be sold through the gift store downstairs, especially if the hospital received a cut of revenue.

Green Landscaping

Anything green is trendy now, and there is no end in sight for this trend. Environmental concerns have never been stronger than they are today. For the small entrepreneur, there are many ways to capitalize on the desire to decrease pollution and environmental damage. Another simple and easy-to-start business would be a green landscaping company. This company would use only environmentally safe chemicals that would perform the necessary weed-killing services but in no way harm the environment or the water table upon which we all rely. Existing landscaping companies should make the switch to green now and should market this as one of their primary benefits, both to the customer and to the world at large.

Green Janitorial Service

Just as with landscaping, consumers see a benefit in using green products for everyday chores. A green housecleaning or commercial janitorial service would offer many benefits to the consumer. With allergies and asthma on the rise, these companies would flourish by marketing their environmental safety. Large office buildings or industrial parks that adopt green janitorial services could market this idea to potential clients as a substantial benefit of the property, just like good parking and security. These businesses would be easy to start, require very little capital, and are in a great niche for future growth.

Consulting

It's always possible for a fifty-year-old executive who is laid off after working for the same company for twenty-five years to stay in the same industry and start a consulting firm. With large and small companies trying to cut costs, any executive with good ideas on proper management techniques and ways to reduce costs and build sales should have a leg up in the consulting industry. We love entrepreneurs who have tons of experience in their field, and even though most entrepreneurs start off in their twenties or thirties, there is no reason why a fifty-year-old should not use his or her talents to help rebuild American industry today. A consulting business requires virtually no startup capital and can rely on very low overhead as both a marketing tool and a financial asset.

Video Editing

Digital media is one of the hot buzzwords in technology today. Certainly, one of the uses that should appeal to our beginning entrepreneurs is the digitalization of existing analog media. Everyone has digital pictures, old home movies, and other forms of family records that would be more enjoyable if they were in a digital format. One of the more popular uses for digital media today is to convert videos and photos into a new movie format. This is a great business for a technologically savvy computer user who is comfortable with movie-editing software.

Smartphone Apps

One of the hottest markets today is the sale of applications created for iPhones and other smartphones. These apps are tiny pieces of software that allow the phones to play games, access stock market quotes, or do any of the other cool things you have seen in the ads. Each app sells for anywhere from $0.99 to $20 via the website portals supported by the phone companies.

Several business models can come from this new market space. One is the development of applications for different phones. Successful apps can easily generate $1 million in sales.

Local Version of Webvan

You may remember the great launch of Webvan, which delivered groceries directly to your house with no delivery fee and no tipping allowed. The company failed, and several hundred million dollars went down the drain for a company we all thought should work. Everyone who used Webvan's service loved it, and its customers were very loyal. But the company made some huge mistakes that have become the fodder for textbooks about business failure. In contrast, England's Tesco grocery store chain has succeeded and even thrived in the same service industry. Tesco delivers, not from one huge central warehouse as Webvan did, but from the store closest to the customer's home. A store employee goes through the aisles, simultaneously packing three or four orders, which are then given to a driver, who delivers them three or four miles to the consumer's house.

This business idea is very simple and could be started with just a minimal investment and only two employees. Simply use the Tesco model of having one person pack orders and another person deliver them. Build a website for a particular neighborhood or even just one zip code.

Another approach involves buying produce and meat directly from farmers and delivering it to consumers at their homes. Fresh-Direct has been successful with this approach in New York City area. Why not study its business model, copy it, and improve it for your city? Remember our earlier advice: it's OK to copy.

Niche Delivery Business

Many small businesses cannot afford to offer delivery services—certain flower shops, for example. Everyone expects that a flower shop will be able to deliver flowers, but mostly only the larger shops are able to do so. The same is true with dry cleaners. So the business proposal here is to go to four or five small florists or dry cleaners and offer to make the deliveries for all of them. Charging each florist $2 or $3 per delivery can be a very profitable business. This would be a great business for a college student or anyone who is willing to work hard five or six hours per day. With almost no startup costs or risk, this business is truly a great one, because there is also no marketing. You let the florist or the dry cleaner do the marketing for you; all you do is deliver the goods.

Pet Care

Pets and pet supplies are a several billion dollar a year industry. But pet owners are always complaining about needing to have someone check in on their pets or take care of their pets when they go away for a long weekend vacation. Advertise in a neighborhood where you are able to walk dogs in the evening and pet-sit during weekends and other vacations. Pet sitters do not need to be with the pet twenty-four hours a day but simply should visit with the customer's pet three or four times a day. Each visit would include a feeding, a bathroom visit, and some playtime for the animal, and you can charge quite a bit more than you would think for these services. This business proposal is very simple and requires almost no startup capital.

Wedding and Event Planner

One of the easiest businesses to start is a wedding- or event-planning business. It requires almost no previous experience, no investment capital, and no licenses or permits. Accordingly, the barriers to entry are very low, and it is very easy for new competitors to join the industry. This business is the ideal choice for many people, especially those who enjoy the world of weddings and being involved in parties. You can work from home, set your own hours, and still lead a normal life or even hold a daytime job while you plan events on the side. To get started, you just need some business cards and one client. This is something you can build gradually by starting with one friend, helping another friend later, and slowly building a clientele and a history of performing well and creating beautiful, fun parties.

Gourmet Health Food Meal Delivery

In the past year or so, several retail establishments have started offering gourmet pickup and meal preparation services. You go to these retail stores and make meals for the upcoming week and month. You carry them home in plastic bags, freeze them, and then do the final cooking when you are ready to eat the meal. This removes several steps in the normal cooking process, such as shopping and selecting recipes, since the retail store does this work for you. However you still have to go to the shop, make the meal, and carry it home.

This business plan goes one step further. You could open a business where the clients sign onto a website and select meals for the week or for the month, and then you bring the completed meals to each client's doorstep, ready to be either frozen or cooked immediately. There is literally nothing for clients to do except to warm up dinner. This business has several different unique marketing platforms, such as ease and help. Not only would you stress the time savings that clients would enjoy, but you would also be able to stress the incredible benefits of offering such healthy food. Also, there would be the opportunity to avoid certain allergies or accommodate certain religious preferences.

Creative Direct Mail

Direct mail has been with us for decades now, so everyone is used to the worthless junk we get in the mail, and marketers are used to the very low 1 or 2 percent response rate. Some companies today are taking direct mail to the next step by increasing the expense of the item sent to all of the potential customers. Instead of simply sending a form letter or a postcard advertising their product, companies are actually sending sample products or small gifts somehow associated with the product or service being advertised. For example, at the most basic level, a fix-it company may send out a small refrigerator magnet printed with the company's telephone number.

This business plan proposes grouping together several direct-mail campaigns and sending out a whole box full of related trinkets or gifts. The boxes would come in bright colors with cool enclosures that all tie together in a symbolic way to represent the products. While this is not popular yet in the United States, many companies in Japan and Europe are having success with this sort of high-value direct-mail campaign, sometimes getting response rates as high as 10 to 15 percent. The cost of starting a business such as this should be very low, since there are few startup expenses.

Organic Baby Food

As more and more parents become convinced of the benefits of healthful eating and organic lifestyles, the demand for organic food has grown exponentially. Some of the baby food companies have tried to keep up, but it's hard to convince a parent that food from a grocery shelf is as healthy as food from a local manufacturer. This plan suggests buying food locally to be cooked into high-quality baby food for families. The food could either be delivered by the company or picked up by the parent, depending on the level of service that the owner wishes to provide. The true added value comes not from delivery but from providing very fresh organic food for children. The website would be created for ordering and for menu selection, and it would also allow the customer to avoid allergy and religious concerns.

Dog-Friendly Coffee Shop

We love our pets. There are tens of millions of dog owners in the United States alone, and these dogs are usually treated as valuable members of the family. Pet specialty companies have proven beyond a doubt that pet owners are willing to pay an extraordinary amount for pet toys, food, and even clothing.

A dog-friendly coffee shop is simply a restaurant for humans with a play area for dogs on the outside. Unlike most restaurants, where pets are not welcomed, this restaurant will welcome pets and even encourage customers to bring them. There will be special treats for dogs—dog cakes and biscuits and anything a dog might enjoy. Outdoors, there is usually a sitting area for the dog owners in a large fenced-in area for all of the various dogs to play and run.

College Travel Company

There are already many college-based travel agencies, companies that provide spring break packages to Daytona Beach and offer study-abroad services to Europe. This idea would serve a different niche altogether. Fraternities and sororities frequently travel en masse, the entire group of one hundred to two hundred members going to a football game or other event. The social director of the fraternity or sorority is in charge of planning the event for the entire group and must arrange meals, buses, tickets, and hotel rooms for the entire group. In this business, you would go to the social directors and offer to plan entire functions for them, so they have absolutely nothing to do but to receive the credit for a job well done. Profit margins would come just as any other travel agency makes its profits, and the startup capital and risks should be very small.

Name Change Service for New Brides

This new business proposes a service for recently married women. When a woman gets married, there are dozens of different forms to fill out and name change requests to be made. The service will change the bride's name on her driver's license, all insurance documents, all credit cards, and anything else the bride would need. This incredibly low-cost business would be simple to start, and the profit margins would increase dramatically, as the process could be done in bulk. For example, one day a week, the entrepreneur would go to city hall and change ten women's names at one time. Advertising could be done on wedding websites and to wedding coordinators, with a small brochure placed at wedding shops and any other places where brides may be shopping.

Liaison Between Local Farmers and Restaurants

We all love fresh fruits and vegetables, and we all love to support local farmers. But only the very best restaurants specialize in using exclusively locally grown produce and other food supplies. This business is a win-win for consumers, farmers, and restaurants. The business will act as a matchmaker between growers and restaurants by going into the community, finding local growers, and then selling the growers' produce to area restaurants. This food distribution business will never actually take ownership of the produce but instead will charge 8 percent of the items sold for the matchmaking service.

Local Lessons

All parents want their kids to take lessons in art, dancing, etiquette, sports, and music. But where do you go to find local piano teachers and to see which ones are the best at what they do? You could start a website that lists all of the local teachers who offer after-school lessons for students and adults. All categories of lessons would be available for listing, thereby creating a networking site for anyone who wants private instruction in any area. The business would earn revenue by charging each instructor a listing fee. And because a site like this would serve a fairly narrow geographic audience, there should be a good market for local advertising on this website as well—say, for used pianos or items such as art supplies or sports equipment that customers would need for lessons offered on the website.

Index

Accountants, 132
ACE. *See* American Computer Experience
Administration, 132–33
Advances, getting, 58–59
Advertising
    on college notebooks, 176
    with GoogleAds, 75–76
    types of, 115
    word-of-mouth, 57, 110, 115
Advisory board, creating an, 135–38
AIG, v
AJC International, 20, 52
Allison, Gerald, 20
Alpert, Terri, 31–32, 78
Amazon.com, 152
American Computer Experience (ACE),
    10–11, 17–18, 42–45, 49, 52, 54–55, 58,
    101, 111–12
American products, exporting, 66
Americana (trade show), 174
Apple Computer, 56, 60
Appraisals, 150, 153–55
Apps, smartphone, 179
Argentina, 72–76
Arie, India, 86
Austria, 77
Automobile repair business, 25

Baby food, organic, 183
Baby furniture rental, 173–74
Back Forty Beer Company, 23–24
Backlinks, 89
Bank loans, 47–48, 141
Bar for locals example, 22–23, 104
Beach, Jim, vi, xii, xv, 56, 85, 132, 134
    and ACE, 10–11, 17–18, 42–45, 49, 52,
        54–55, 58, 101, 111–12
    advisory board created by, 137–38
    and business valuation, 150
    entrepreneurship class of, 2–6
    leather-good import business of class of,
        72–77
Bear Stearns, v
Beer brewing, 23–24
Benefits of product or service, focusing on,
    113
Best Buy, 82

BizBuySell, 139
Blogs, 121
Bootstrapping, 41–61
    definition of, 12
    and impossibility of predicting success,
        42–45
    raising capital vs., 45–50
    rules of, 50–61
Brainstorming, 38–39, 95
Brand names, associating with others',
    54–55
Brazil, 72
Brides, name change service for new,
    184–85
Brokers, franchise, 147
Brown, Quinn, xii
Brown, Randy, xi–xv, 127
Brown, Zac, 86
Buenos Aires, Argentina, 72
Burn rate, 50
Business plans, 41–44, 60–61
Buying a business, 139–48
    advantages of, 142–43
    disadvantages of, 143–44
    franchising, 144–48
    with no money down, 139–42

Capital, raising, 45–50, 150
Capital Group (UPS), 58
Cash flow, 54, 155
Cashing out, 162–64
Chambers of Commerce, 162
Chang, Henry, 82–83
Chick-fil-A, 146–47
Children, passing the business to your, 163
China, 58, 60, 79
CIMA, 73
Clichés, avoiding, 113
Coca-Cola, 19, 106, 121
Coffee shop, dog-friendly, 183–84
Cold calling, 115
Collective Soul, 86
College notebooks, ads for, 176
College travel company, 184
Commission-only salespeople, 133
Commodity businesses, 100
Competitive advantage, 94

Consulting, 178–79
Contracts, 141, 148
Copying other businesses, 34–35
Corporate culture, 134
Corridor principle, 68–69
Craigslist, 86
Creative direct mail, 182–83
Creativity, 19, 35–39
  and brainstorming, 38–39
  as learned skill, 36
Credibility, establishing, 102–3
Cultural issues (international business), 67
Culture, business, 98–99, 134, 143
Current occupation, re-creating your,
  20–21
Customer experience, the, 92–94, 97
Customers
  being honest with, 54
  getting advances from, 58–59
  getting ideas from your, 59
  identifying wants of, 102
  initial skepticism of, 103

David, Anthony, 86
Davis, Tamar, 86
Day job, keeping your, vii–ix, xiii, 56,
  157–59
Dealer, becoming a, 33–34
Decision, success as a, 9
Delivery business, niche, 180–81
Dell, Michael, 55–56
Deposits, getting, 58–59
Differentiation, value-based, 97, 104
Digital media, 179
Dinner, exploring business ideas over, 37
Direct mail, 115–16, 182–83
DOC. See U.S. Department of Commerce
Dog-friendly coffee shop, 183–84
Domain name registration sites, 3
Dot-coms, 152
Down economy, starting a business in a,
  10–13
Dreamweaver, 85
Drive to succeed, 9
Drop shipping, 119–25
  definition of, 119
  disadvantages of, 123–25
  as lifestyle business, 131
  and product selection, 120–22
  and selecting a drop shipper, 122–23

Economy, starting a business in a down,
  10–13
Elance, 176
Elevator pitch, 111
Ellison, Larry, 2
Emotions, identifying with your customers',
  105–6
Employee(s)
  costs associated with, 128, 130–31,
    158–59
  essential, 132–33
  hiring (see Hiring)
  selling the business to your, 163–64

Ending your business
  by selling it, 162–64
  and succession planning, 164–66
Entrepreneur, 35
Entrepreneur School, The, 88, 89, 110, 122,
  167, 170
Entrepreneurship
  avoiding wasted time with, ix–x
  as different path, vi
  efficiency of, xi
  as learnable skill, 1
  low-risk, vi–vii
  physical and mental benefits of, xiv
EPR Creations, 86
Equity stakes, offering, 133
Event planning, 181
Export.gov, 66
Extreme sports website, 83

Facebook, 110–11, 152, 175
Fear of the unknown, 64, 72
Feldman, Ben, 29–30, 51, 78
Financial transactions, international,
  64–65
Financing
  as curse, 12
  from outside sources, 150
  seller, 140
Fitness center example, 112–13
Flooring business example, 101–2, 114
Food and Wine magazine, 32
Ford Taurus, 102–3
Forecasting from the bottom up, 59
Foreclosed-property management, 175
Franchise Direct, 146
Franchising, 144–48
Free labor, utilizing, 57–58
FreshDirect, 180
Friends and family, getting help from, 48,
  134
Funding, external, 45–50
Furniture Origins, 77–79

Galloway, Jeff, 26–27, 78
Galloway Productions, 27
Galloway School, 26
Gates, Bill, 2, 47
Gatsby (Japanese product), 38
General Motors, v
Georgia State University, xii, 2
Getting operational, 51
Gift Creations, 169
Gladwell, Malcolm, 28
Global Entrepreneurship Monitor, 17
Global Pet Expo, 30
GoDaddy.com, 4
Gold Key Service, 3
Goodwill Games, 11
Google rankings, 88–89
Google Toolbar, 88
GoogleAds, 75–76, 87, 110
Gourmet health food meal delivery,
  182
Great American Beer Festival, 24

Green janitorial service, 178
Green landscaping, 177–78
Green products, 174
Grocery delivery service, 179–80
Growing slowly, 53, 56
Growth, limits on, 128

Haggling, 56–57
Hanks, Chris, vi, xii, xv, 85, 135
    and story of three-level bar idea, 46
    advisory board created by, 137
    and business valuation, 150
    first business of, 10
    and flooring franchise client, 101–2
    janitorial service business of, 139–40
    on niches, 30
    painting business of, 97–99, 145, 146
    Vietnam truck business of, 68–71, 101
Health insurance, 161–62
Health issues, 16
Hewlett-Packard, 55
High-value products, offering, 52–53
Hiring
    avoiding mistakes in, 134
    and building a team, 127–30
    and business growth, 158–59
    and determining need for employees,
        130–32
    in a down economy, 13
    key areas for, 132–33
Home, starting your business at, 55–56
Honest, being, 54
Hong Kong Trade Association, 86
Hospital spa services, 177
Hotels, delivery for, 177

Idea(s)
    acting on your, 33
    and creativity, 36
    jotting down, 37–38
    uniqueness of your, 16–18
Import/export opportunities, looking for, 58.
    See also International business(es)
Inc. magazine, 35
Incorporation, 44–45
India, online tutoring from, 176
Indonesia, 78
Infinovate, 21
In-house, doing things, 55
Inspiration, providing, 130
Intel, 18, 55
Internal funds, using, 47
Internal Revenue Service, 45
International business(es), 63–79
    cultural issues with, 67
    Erik Rostad example, 84–87
    fears about starting an, 64–65
    Furniture Origins example, 77–79
    getting started in, 65–66
    paths to, 63–64
    service, exporting a, 67–71
    small players, dealing with, 71–77
    Timeless Chair example, 2–7
International Entrepreneurship, 66

Internet
    international sales via, 65
    marketing on the, 109–11
Internet businesses
    discounted technology example, 82–83
    with drop shipping, 120–22
    Erik Rostad's success in, 84–87
    and search engine optimization (SEO),
        87–89
    and sticky websites, 83–84
Internships, 57–58
Investors, outside, 48

Janitorial service
    business example, 139–40
    green, 178
Japan, 38, 52, 58, 66, 183
Japan External Trade Organization, 58,
    66
Joiner, Eric, 20, 52, 78–79
Jutan, Seth, 77–78

Kawasaki, Guy, 60

Lady Gaga, 103
Landscaping, green, 177–78
Lawn-care business example, 92–93, 106
Leather-good importing business, 72–77
Lehman Brothers, v
Lessons, local, 185
Letters of credit, 70
Lifestyle businesses, 131
Lines of credit, 52
LinkedIn, 136
Loans, 52
Locals' bar example, 22–23, 104
Local farmers, liaison between restaurants
    and, 185
Locke, Gary, 71
Lockheed, 20
Logos, getting access to famous, 121
Low-risk entrepreneurship, vi–vii

Manager, hiring a, 159
Manufacturing, 60
Marketing, 109–17
    developing tactics for, 114–17
    as essential function, 132
    and getting your message right, 111–14
    identifying your target market, 114–17
    on the Internet, 109–11
    secondary impacts, 116
Massachusetts Institute of Technology
    (MIT), 17, 18, 42–43, 54–55, 101
Meal delivery service, gourmet health food,
    182
Mental image of your business, creating a,
    104–5
Microsoft, 18, 55, 159
Money
    raising, 45–50
    spending, 44, 49
Moonlight kitchen, 176
Morgan Stanley, 31

Multiple businesses, starting, ix, 86–87,
    159–62
Murphy, Doug, 11, 17–18, 42–45, 49, 52,
    54–56, 58, 111–12, 132, 134
Musical performance, 86
Myths about entrepreneurship, 9–18
    genetic trait, success is a, 1, 9
    good economy, companies thrive only in
        a, 10
    risk takers, entrepreneurs are all, 13
    unique idea, you need a, 16

Name change service, 184–85
National Collegiate Athletic Association
    (NCAA), 121
National Football League (NFL), 121
Negativity, avoiding, 39
Niche delivery business, 180–81
Niches, 30
Nike, 26
No money down, buying a business with,
    139–42
Northeastern University, 86
Notepad, carrying around a, 37

Occupation, re-creating your current,
    20–21
Ocean-freight auditing business, 51
oDesk, 176
Offshore partner, finding an, 68
Online tutoring, 176
Operations, 132
Options pools, 130
Organic baby food, 183
Organic growth, 53
Others, learning from, 16–18
Outside funding, 47–50

Page rank (PR), 88–89, 122
Painting business example, 97–99, 145, 146
Pakistan, 2–5
Paraguay, 66
Passion
    about your product, 26
    following your, 21–26
Patient Protection and Affordable Care Act,
    161
Paulson, Betty, 31
Paulson, Paul, 30–31
Paying yourself, 56
Pepsi-Cola Company, 19
Peru, 85
Pet care, 181
Phidippides, 26–27
Planning
    for success, 42–45, 60–61
    succession, 164–66
PR (page rank), 88–89, 122
Pressure blankets for dogs, 30
Price(s)
    arguing, 56–57
    competing on, 100–101
    perfect, 111
    value vs., 150–53
Problems, solving, 29–33, 91
Professional Cutlery Direct, 32

Profit
    cash vs., 54
    forecasting your, 59, 114
    reinvesting your, 158
Profitability, and value, 152
Property management, foreclosed, 175
Public relations efforts, 115

Quick sales, looking for, 52
QuickBooks, 132

Receivables, 52
Recession, v
Recipe kiosks, 174
Register.com, 4
Reid, Tierra, 167–72
Relevant, being, 104
Reputation, business, 143
Research
    letting your customers fund your, 59
    taking advantage of big companies cutting
        back on, 13
RestaurantOwner.com, 22
Restaurants
    liaison between local farmers and, 185
    startup costs for, 47
Retirement, 164
Revenue streams, creating multiple, 69
Ride sharing, social network for, 175
Risk
    health, 16
    lost time as, 15–16
    reducing, 13–15
Rostad, Erik, 84–88
Russell Corporation, 84–85
Russia, 66
Ruth's Chris Steak House, 99

Sales, focusing on, 111
Sales goals, setting, 59
Salesperson(s)
    being your own, 55
    commission-only, 133
Saudi Arabia, 67
Scheduling, 98
Search engine optimization (SEO), 87–89
Secondary marketing impacts, 116
Seller financing, buying a business with,
    140
Selling what sells, 101–2
Selling your business, 162–64
SEO (search engine optimization), 87–89
Service, exporting a, 67–71
Service businesses, 60
ServiceMagic, 116
Ship first, then test, 60
Shipping containers, 5
Silly Bandz, 29
Simpson, Catherine, 24–25
Skepticism, 103
SkinLeather.com, 73
Skype, 176
Small Business Administration, 170
Smartphone apps, 179
Social networking, 175
Solving a problem, 29–33

South Korea, 72
Spa services, hospital, 177
Sporting goods store, 26–27
Sports merchandise example, 120–21, 124
Stahl, David, 20–21, 53
Stanford University, 17, 18, 42–43, 54–55, 101
Statistics, using, 103, 113
Sticky websites, 83–84, 121–22
Stine, Cherie, 28–29, 58, 59, 79
Stretchy Shapes, 28–29
Stump grinding, 31
Stylish Consignments, 168
Succeed, drive to, 9
Success
    as a decision, 9
    myths about, 1, 9
    planning for, 42–45, 60–61
Succession planning, 164–66
Support team, doing without a, 53
SurgeryU, 86
Swatch, 55

Target market, identifying your, 100
Tatum, Joey, 22–23, 47, 104
Team, building a, 127–30
Temporary workers, using, 131
Tesco, 180
Testing
    of marketing techniques, 114
    of your value proposition, 99–107
Three-level bar example, 46–47
Time, lost, 15–16
Timeless Chair, 2–7, 72
Tipping Point, The (Malcolm Gladwell), 28
Trade shows, 73, 74, 111, 146
Transferable skills, 134
Trends, focusing on, 28
Trial and error, xiii
Turner, Ted, 11
Tutoring, online, 176
Twitter, 57, 152

Understaffing, 53
Unemployment, v
Unexpected, being, 107
Uniqueness of your idea, 16–18

Unknown, fear of the, 64, 72
UPS, 58, 66, 88
Uruguay, 66
U.S. Commercial Service, 71
U.S. Department of Commerce (DOC), 3, 66, 71

Vacations, getting ideas during, 38
Valuation companies, 153–54
Value of your business, 149–55
    approaches to determining, 154–55
    maximizing, 155
    and outside financing, 150
    valuation companies for determining, 153–54
    and value vs. price, 150–53
Value proposition
    creating your, 94–99
    and customer experience, 92–94
    refining your, 100
    rules for testing your, 99–107
    and "wow" factor, 91
Venture capital, 48, 78
VeriSign, 78
Video editing, 179
Vietnam, 68–71, 101
Vision, providing, 130

Walmart, 53, 100
Waste Management Inc., 29
We, using the royal, 57
Wealth, creating, 128
Websites
    drop-shipping, 120–22
    and search engine optimization, 87–89
    sticky, 83–84, 121–22
Webvan, 179–80
Wedding planning, 181
Welch, Jack, on competitive advantage, 94
Wilson, Jason, 23–24
Winfrey, Oprah, 2
Word-of-mouth advertising, 57, 110, 115
Workplace, wastefulness of modern, ix–x
Worn phrases, avoiding, 113
"Wow" factor, 91, 106–7

Yard signs, 115

With the purchase of this book, you are entitled to a month's free membership on our website, *www.TheEntrepreneurSchool.com.*

On the website, you can learn more about many of the topics covered in the book, get access to our webinars, hear directly from the characters in this book, and get advice from other entrepreneurs like yourself.

The site requires that you register and sign in.
When you are asked for a code, enter **startup** *(lowercase, one word).*

1 2 3 4 5 6 7 8 9 10 11 12 13 14 15 DOC/DOC 1 9 8 7 6 5 4 3 2 1

ISBN   978-0-07-175393-7
MHID   0-07-175393-1

e-ISBN   978-0-07-176174-1
e-MHID   0-07-176174-8

This publication is designed to provide accurate and authoritative information in regard to the subject matter covered. It is sold with the understanding that neither the author nor the publisher is engaged in rendering legal, accounting, securities trading, or other professional services. If legal advice or other expert assistance is required, the services of a competent professional person should be sought.

—*From a Declaration of Principles Jointly Adopted by a Committee of the American Bar Association and a Committee of Publishers and Associations*

Library of Congress Cataloging-in-Publication Data

Beach, Jim (James)
    School for startups : the breakthrough course for guaranteeing small business success in 90 days or less / by Jim Beach, Chris Hanks, and David Beasley.
        p.   cm.
    Includes index.
    ISBN 978-0-07-175393-7 (alk. paper)
        1. New business enterprises—Management.   2. Small business—Management.   3. Entrepreneurship.   I. Hanks, Chris.   II. Beasley, David.   III. Title.

    HD62.5.B43   2011
    658.1′1—dc22   2011008758

SCHOOL FOR STARTUPS

The Breakthrough Course
for Guaranteeing
Small Business Success
in 90 Days or Less

Jim Beach,
Chris Hanks,
and David Beasley

Mc
Graw
Hill

New York   Chicago   San Francisco   Lisbon   London   Madrid   Mexico City
Milan   New Delhi   San Juan   Seoul   Singapore   Sydney   Toronto